PRAISE FOR
ARROW STRIKER

"I can boldly say you'll be stronger in your faith after reading *Arrow Striker*. This book will inspire you to greater Christian commitment as you step into the opportunities God has for you. We need this message now more than ever!"

—MARK BATTERSON, *NEW YORK TIMES* BEST-SELLING AUTHOR OF *THE CIRCLE MAKER* AND LEAD PASTOR, NATIONAL COMMUNITY CHURCH

"Contrary to what most people think, an extraordinary life isn't the result of a passionate pursuit for significance. Rather, it's the natural result of a life lived with ordinary day-to-day decisions based on a clear purpose and mission. In *Arrow Striker*, Jonathan Hardy shows what that path looks like with biblical insights, practical tips, and real-life examples."

—LARRY OSBORNE, AUTHOR AND TEACHING PASTOR, NORTH COAST CHURCH

"*Arrow Striker* is an incredibly encouraging book that will impact how you live each day—helping you understand and embrace all that God intended your life to be. The words within these pages will challenge and empower you to live out your divine purpose and use your unique gifts and talents to impact the people around you and change the world!"

—DEBBIE LINDELL, LEAD PASTOR, JAMES RIVER CHURCH AND AUTHOR OF *SHE PRAYS*

"Jonathan Hardy reminds you that God has a specific plan for your life regardless of where you're at on the journey. He helps you understand how God can use your unique giftings and everyday interactions to make your mark on those in your sphere of influence. Enjoy the read and spiritual piercing of *Arrow Striker*."

—DOUG CLAY, GENERAL SUPERINTENDENT,
THE ASSEMBLIES OF GOD USA

"World changers don't develop overnight...but they do develop. Jonathan Hardy has written an inspirational book that challenges Christians to step into God-ordained opportunities to impact those in their spheres of influence. Upon reading this book, you'll see new ways to impact those around you right here, right now."

—ROB KETTERLING, LEAD PASTOR, RIVER VALLEY CHURCH AND
AUTHOR OF *FRONT ROW LEADER* AND *SPEED OF UNITY*

"When I saw the title *Arrow Striker*, it made me wonder, "What is that?" But after Jonathan's refresher on that great 2 Kings 13 account, it makes me want to keep striking my arrows every day in order to accomplish God's will in my life."

—KENT INGLE, PRESIDENT, SOUTHEASTERN UNIVERSITY AND
AUTHOR OF *FRAMEWORK LEADERSHIP* AND *MODERN GUIDE TO COLLEGE*

"While the enemy of our souls wants to minimize our effectiveness as believers, God wants people to experience abundant life. That's why I can't wait for people to read *Arrow Striker*! As you step into what God has for you each day, God will bless your life far beyond what you could've ever imagined. Everyone needs to read this book!"

—SCOTT WILSON, GLOBAL PASTOR, OAKS CHURCH AND
AUTHOR OF *IMPACT: RELEASING THE POWER OF INFLUENCE*

"Jonathan does a masterful job helping us see how our actions can lead to greater influence and impact among our friends, co-workers, neighbors, and community. After reading this book, I am confident you'll want to give a wholehearted pursuit toward fulfilling God's desires for your own life."

—CALEB CHAMBERS, SHOALS CAMPUS PASTOR,
CHURCH OF THE HIGHLANDS

"In his book *Arrow Striker*, Jonathan Hardy reminds us that the everyday circumstances of our lives aren't accidental or insignificant, but rather divinely orchestrated opportunities to make a lasting impact in the lives of people around us. Thank you, Jonathan, for such a powerful and inspiring resource that builds up the body of Christ and advances the gospel."

—KRISTEN FEOLA, AUTHOR OF *THE ULTIMATE GUIDE TO THE DANIEL FAST*

"Great job, Jonathan. *Arrow Striker* will challenge everyone who's serious about giving it all for God. Well done, easy to read, and practical to apply."

—CHRIS RAILEY, LEAD PASTOR, OAKS CHURCH

"I've known Jonathan Hardy for more than twenty years, and I can attest to his love for people and desire to encourage the body of Christ. As you read *Arrow Striker*, you'll get an up-close and personal look from a man who lives by his word. As you read the pages of this book, I'm confident you'll be inspired to wholeheartedly live out your faith with passion and enthusiasm."

—SCOTTY GIBBONS, LEAD PASTOR, PEOPLE'S CHURCH

"Jonathan Hardy is a personal friend. This book has been on his heart and mind for years, and I'm so glad it's finally available for you to read. I can't wait for you to dive into what God has for you as you look to fulfill His plan for your life each day."

—Grant Baldwin, founder, The Speaker Lab and author of *The Successful Speaker*

"I am so grateful Jonathan Hardy has written his first of what I know will be many books to advance the body of Christ. I'm not sure he could have started with a greater subject than for all of us to become arrow strikers. This is a great book that will motivate you to do more for God with greater impact on those around you. This is a must-read!"

—Alejandro Reyes, CEO of Digital Napkin

"Regardless of your past failures or successes, this book can help you step into the next chapter God has for your life. If you want to grab a hold of all God wants to do through you, then buckle up. It's time to get started on an incredible journey where you'll experience a renewed sense of purpose for your life."

—Steve Svoboda, executive pastor of ministries, Oaks Church

"In *Arrow Striker*, you'll see how to find and follow God's leading each day. Get ready for a fantastic journey to experience all God has for your life!"

—Ryan Wakefield, founder, Church Marketing University

"In 2 Kings 13, Elisha encouraged King Jehoash to strike the ground with a handful of arrows—the more the strikes, the greater the victory. Jehoash didn't take full advantage of this opportunity, however. The central lesson of Jonathan Hardy's *Arrow Striker* is, "Don't be like Jehoash!" Instead, use every gift and opportunity you have to extend the influence of God's kingdom. Whether you're a CEO or a stay-at-home parent, you'll find encouragement and practical help in this book."

—GEORGE P. WOOD, EXECUTIVE EDITOR, *INFLUENCE* MAGAZINE

"What I love about *Arrow Striker* is how easy it is to read, and at the same time, how much it pushes me to act. Every chapter sets a challenge before me to go for it. And the best part: Jonathan communicates how to have impact in a way that's easy and practical. I don't think I realized how many ways I can make an even bigger difference right now, without changing anything. I love that. Thank you, Jonathan, for such a great investment in my life!"

—JUSTIN TRAPP, FOUNDER, MINISTRY PASS AND SERMONARY

"Inspired! *Arrow Striker* takes a pragmatic approach to help readers understand the significance of their normal everyday lives for accomplishing God's purposes. Jonathan provides specific examples of how people can use their current gifts, talents, resources, and opportunities to make an impact, whether big or small."

—TYLER SMITH, CO-FOUNDER, TEXT IN CHURCH AND
AUTHOR OF *BOOMERANG*

"The subject matter for *Arrow Striker* has been on the heart of my good friend Jonathan Hardy for several years now. I've often heard him talk about the ideas of trusting God for big things and living a life of no regrets. So as a friend, to see this book come to fruition is an absolute joy! What makes reading this book especially powerful is knowing that Jonathan is a guy who lives what this book teaches. He has consistently trusted God at key points and has seen those moments of faith advance God's kingdom in big ways. In *Arrow*

Striker, he unpacks how you and I can do the same. Your life and faith will be made better by applying the principles in this book."

—SCOTT OBREMSKI, LEAD PASTOR, SUMMIT PARK CHURCH

"This book motivates us to be committed to God's desire for our lives and to step into the types of opportunities we all face from time to time so we can make a considerable difference for the kingdom of God. I highly recommend you get started reading *Arrow Striker* right away."

—CASEY GIBBONS, MOM TO SIX, AUTHOR, SPEAKER

"Jonathan has done an outstanding job communicating how we can do more for God without becoming legalistic. He powerfully describes the sufficiency of Christ in our lives while painting a beautiful picture of how we can express our faith through our deeds and actions. I know you'll enjoy it!"

—JUSTIN LATHROP, VICE PRESIDENT, SOUTHEASTERN UNIVERSITY
AND AUTHOR OF *THE LIKEABLE CHRISTIAN*

"Following Jesus is not a one-size-fits-all approach. All believers are individually gifted to follow God's unique plan for their lives. The concepts Jonathan writes about in *Arrow Striker* will make you want to tap into your unique gifts in pursuit of a full-on effort for Him."

—STEPHEN MADDOX, HEAD OF PRODUCTION, HILLSONG UK

ARROW STRIKER

ARROW STRIKER

Live with Purpose and Leave an Eternal Impact ... Every Single Day

Jonathan Hardy

Published by Leaders.Church
1105 W. Woodbine Street, Springfield, MO 65803
www.leaders.church

Unless otherwise indicated, Scripture quotations are from:
The Holy Bible, New International Version (NIV) © 1973, 1978, 1984, 2011 by Biblica, Inc.™ Used by permission. All rights reserved worldwide.

Other Scripture quotations are from:
Holy Bible, New Living Translation (NLT) © 1996, 2004 by Tyndale Charitable Trust. Used by permission of Tyndale House Publishers. All rights reserved.

The Holy Bible, English Standard Version (ESV) © 2001 by Crossway Bibles, a division of Good News Publishers. Used by permission. All rights reserved.

The Message (MSG) © by Eugene H. Peterson 1993, 1994, 1995, 1996, 2000, 2001, 2002. Used by permission of NavPress Publishing Group.

Some names have been changed to protect the privacy of the individuals involved. While the author has made every effort to provide accurate internet addresses at the time of publication, neither the publisher nor the author assumes any responsibility for errors or for changes that occur after publication. Further, the publisher and author do not have control over and do not assume any responsibility for third-party websites or their content.

Library of Congress Cataloging-in-Publication Data:

An application to register this book for cataloging has been submitted to the Library of Congress.
ISBN: 979-8-9862385-0-0 (paperback)
ISBN: 979-8-9862385-1-7 (ebook)

Printed in the United States of America
22 23 24 25 26 27 — 7 6 5 4 3 2 1

To Ashley
Thank you for your amazing love, encouragement, and insight.
This book would not exist without you.

CONTENTS

CONTENTS

FOREWORD

Pastor John Lindell

Upon following Jesus, it doesn't take us long to realize there's more to life than simply knowing God. Each of us is created and gifted by God to fulfill a unique and powerful purpose. How we respond to that reality is the basis of our gift back to God.

That's why I'm excited that you're reading this book. *Arrow Striker* will help you capture each moment possible and tap into your God-given potential to significantly impact those you encounter on a regular basis.

I first met Jonathan Hardy twenty-one years ago. A few years into our new friendship, Jonathan joined the pastoral staff at James River Church, where he served for seven years. The concept for this book was birthed in Jonathan's heart years ago. I believe that what you're about to read is a much-needed message, and I'm so glad it has finally been released.

This book is not theoretical. It's grounded in lived experience. Jonathan has modeled these principles throughout the twenty-one years I've known him. His practical wisdom and scriptural insight will inspire you to serve God without reservation and to follow Him without hesitation.

Don't just read this book—lean in, learn, and begin to lead a life where you see God use you in ways you never thought possible.

I believe you're embarking on a transformational journey full of God's blessing and promise. The best is yet to come for you as you make His purposes your priority each day!

John Lindell
Lead Pastor, James River Church
Author of *New Normal* and *Soul Set Free*

PART 1

OPPORTUNITY AWAITS

God is always at work. He has a divine master plan that has existed since the beginning of time. Throughout the millennia, He has orchestrated circumstances and events to achieve His will. He's an all-powerful God with the ability to do whatever He wants, whenever He wants. And yet God chooses to use people to accomplish His purposes every single day.

God longs to intimately know people and give them abundant life. He wants them to thrive in their homes, schools, workplaces, and communities. He desires to provide for their every need. And ultimately, He wishes to use them to help, serve, and give to others. He's looking for people just like you who'll live wholeheartedly with purpose and intentionality, no matter where they are on life's journey.

You just never know what God might do through you as you make His purposes a priority. He has a unique plan to use your life regardless of your career, stage of life, spiritual acumen, or past mistakes. As you take small steps forward each day, God can

1

use those actions to make a big difference in the lives of others.

As you'll see in the chapters that follow, God wants to use your small acts of kindness, ordinary conversations, and simple steps of faith to benefit those around you. Opportunity awaits every single day, and God wants you to tap into each opportunity. When you remain faithful to God's purposes, you'll see how you can easily step into opportunities and give a wholehearted effort toward achieving His will each day.

Download a study guide for personal reflection
or group discussion: www.arrowstriker.com/guide

CHAPTER 1

THE ARROW OF VICTORY

Fear gripped the country. Panic prevailed. Mothers trembled, gripping their children as their tears fell on dry ground. They were hiding in mountain caves, whispering prayers for the safety of their husbands and sons who risked their lives to save their families. Death, violence, looting, and slavery—here was their new reality. Every father, mother, son, and daughter would either die or become a slave.

Without warning, any day could be their last on Earth. Would they wake up to see another morning, or was this the end? That was the question everyone was asking.

Until God intervened.

It was the early eighth century BC, and God had a plan to use two men to change the trajectory for the nation of Israel. Facing near extinction, the Israelite army had diminished to virtually nothing because another nation, Aram, had nearly wiped them out.[1] The potential of losing everything left Israel with dwindling hope. Aram was a much more powerful nation, and there was no way the Israelites could defend themselves against their enemy's size and strength, which easily allowed them to commandeer city after city.

Now it was Israel's turn. They were next in line to face this dreadful reality. They had no idea when Aram would return to destroy them for good. However, in a single defining moment, the situation instantly unfolded in Israel's favor—because God was at work behind the scenes.

God planned to use Israel's new king, Jehoash, along with the prophet Elisha, to play integral roles in determining the nation's success. He wanted them to have a significant impact in saving Israel during this perilous time.

As leader of the nation, Jehoash was frightened because he knew Elisha was declining in both age and strength. Elisha's death quickly approached, and Jehoash on his own didn't know how to keep Israel intact and survive Aram's coming invasion. Jehoash loathed the idea of Israel's destruction, especially under his leadership, but what could be done?

All Israel panicked. The nation's future could not have looked bleaker.

That's how serious this moment was.

> God wanted to help them, and He had a battle plan that was humanly unthinkable.

But God wanted to help them, and He had a battle plan that was humanly unthinkable. The prophet Elisha, as messenger for God, had one final moment to encourage the fear-filled king and deliver hope to Israel. Scripture describes this obscure and unconventional message in 2 Kings 13, and it reveals how the king's actions determined the nation's destiny:

> Elisha said, "Get a bow and some arrows," and he
> [Jehoash] did so. "Take the bow in your hands," he
> said to the king of Israel. When he had taken it, Eli-
> sha put his hands on the king's hands. "Open the east
> window," he said, and he opened it. "Shoot!" Elisha
> said, and he shot. "The LORD's arrow of victory, the
> arrow of victory over Aram!" Elisha declared. "You
> will completely destroy the Arameans at Aphek."[2]

Wow, what a message for such a moment!

Jehoash's arrow represented complete and final destruction of Aram. It was truly an arrow of victory. The nation that oppressed Israel for years would actually experience their utter downfall.

Of all the nations, God uniquely planned for Israel to bring about Aram's defeat. And God's plans included not only Aram's defeat in a single battle but also their annihilation.

This news should have resulted in a big celebration. Jehoash had received a message from the man of God himself that victory was imminent. Right then and there, Israel had shifted from powerless to powerful, from loser to winner.

However, something terrible immediately happened. The final message from Elisha turned sour. In a single moment, Jehoash's next response stripped Israel of their ultimate and complete victory. This scripture continues:

> Then he [Elisha] said, "Take the arrows," and the
> king took them. Elisha told him, "Strike the ground."
> He struck it three times and stopped. The man of
> God was angry with him and said, "You should have
> struck the ground five or six times; then you would
> have defeated Aram and completely destroyed it.

But now you will defeat it only three times." Elisha died and was buried.[3]

This is crazy, isn't it? Elisha instructed Jehoash to literally grab the set of arrows in his hand and hit the ground with them. Such a command is beyond unconventional.

Jehoash complied—but not to the extent Elisha desired. Had he kept striking the ground, Israel could have celebrated one of its greatest victories of all time. The history books would have read: *Powerless Israel Conquers Superpower Forever*. Instead, Israel would be victorious only to a degree—they would win three battles, but they wouldn't permanently destroy Aram.

Elisha concluded his life attempting to give hope to Israel, while Jehoash's actions yielded a different destiny.

Jehoash lacked enthusiasm for accomplishing the task at hand. Did he really believe they would wipe out Aram? Did his hope waver? Did he lack trust in Elisha and his instructions? Did fear and worry prevent him from fulfilling God's plan for Israel? The king gave a half-hearted effort to this incredible opportunity, and as a result, he missed out on what God wanted to do through him to accomplish an extraordinary victory for the nation.

But Elisha did all he could to give Israel a complete and total victory. He was sick and approaching death, yet he still allowed God to use him to the very end—by giving an encouraging word and imparting the power of God to the king—literally doing all he could for God in those last moments of his life on Earth. Elisha believed God would give Israel the victory, and he committed the entirety of his life to accomplishing God's purposes.

CHAPTER 2

ARROW STRIKERS

As a child in the 1980s, I heard the song "I'm in the Lord's Army" every single week in Sunday school. If you didn't have the privilege of growing up in church back then, you missed out. But since we live in the day when information is available at our fingertips, I give you permission to pull up a quick search for it right now. You're welcome.

Many of the songs in "kids church" contained deep theological concepts. This particular song's lyrics simply said,

> *I may never march in the infantry,*
> *ride in the cavalry, shoot the artillery;*
> *I may never fly o'er the enemy,*
> *but I'm in the Lord's army.*

At the time, I didn't grasp the meaning of that song. I knew what it referred to, but at a young age, I don't think I understood its significance. As silly as that song feels today, it has profound truth for the way we should view our lives.

In reality, we live in a spiritual battle. We rarely think about this life as a battle, but the apostle Paul alluded to this when he said, "Put on the full armor of God, so that you can take your stand against the devil's schemes. For our struggle is not against flesh and blood, but against the rulers, against the authorities, against the powers of this dark world and against the spiritual forces of evil in the heavenly realms."[4]

This life is a battle of good versus evil, light versus darkness, and heaven versus hell. There are spiritual forces at work against the good that God wants to accomplish in our lives. The enemy wants to separate people from God. He wants to minimize believers' impact. He wants to ruin their lives.

The spiritual battle is real. The enemy has clearly waged war against God and humanity, but there's more to the story. God will have the ultimate victory, and He wants to use *us* to participate in that victory.

You've Been Drafted

In the fall of 1940, the United States government instituted the Selective Training and Service Act, which required all men between the ages of twenty-one and thirty-six to register for the draft. This was the first peacetime draft in U.S. history. Variations to this act developed throughout the decades that followed, and parts of it still exist today. The most notable component that no longer applies today is the required military enlistment—the U.S. currently has a 100 percent volunteer military service.

But the draft in God's spiritual military is fully operational—and *you* have been drafted. Like it or not, you entered the spiritual war at birth, and you're in it every single day. As Pastor John Lindell articulates it, "We are born into war, each of us children of a cosmic conflict."[5]

You are an active-duty soldier in the spiritual battle. But most people don't think about it that way. They don't live like they're in battle, and they don't view themselves as soldiers. Since the majority of citizens don't enlist in the military, they don't know what it's like to be a soldier. The idea of a "spiritual soldier" seems incomprehensible or unrelatable.

Having never been in the military myself, I can't fully grasp the realities of physical war and what the life of a soldier, sailor, airman, coast guardsman, or marine is like. That's why I often ask my friends about their war experiences. When in the military, soldiers serve their country. They serve their commander. They support and care for their comrades. They sacrifice their personal desires and preferences to accomplish the mission given to them.

The mindset, lifestyle, and behavior of military personnel epitomize how to live the Christian life. You have a mission to accomplish—orders from God Almighty—to make a difference and leave an eternal impact every single day. Your life isn't about just you. The amount of money you make, the accolades you receive, and the accomplishments you achieve mean nothing if you don't complete the mission of God.

The apostle Paul understood this reality. In his letter to Philemon, he referred to a man named Archippus as a "fellow soldier" because he grasped the unseen battle taking place in the spiritual realm. These early church leaders viewed themselves as soldiers in God's spiritual military, with missions to accomplish. When writing to Archippus, Paul gave him this specific encouragement:

"See to it that you complete the work you have received in the Lord."[6]

Archippus had a work to complete. If Paul were alive today, he'd say the same thing to you and me. God has a work He wants you to complete. He wants to use your life every single day. He wants to give you daily opportunities to make a difference by fighting this spiritual battle. The question is, how will you fight?

Sometimes people miss opportunities or fail to accomplish God's purposes because they don't look at their daily life as a mission from God. The spiritual forces want to distract us from our assignments, to steer us off track, and ultimately to stop us from making the most of our daily, God-given opportunities.

The enemy longs to minimize your influence on others and your impact for God's kingdom. The apostle Peter put it this way: "Your enemy the devil prowls around like a roaring lion looking for someone to devour."[7] Satan not only wants to minimize your impact, but he actually wants to devour you. He wants to eat up your potential. Frankly, he doesn't want you to exist. He wants you to finish life with no influence, no impact, and no legacy.

But I have good news. God wants you to maximize your life, to make the most of every opportunity, and to leave a lasting impact on those around you. Just as God sent Jesus into the world, He has now sent you into the world. He wants you to help those far from Him to find life in Him. He wants you to reach people, serve people, encourage people, and help people. He wants you to engage in the spiritual battle.

Looking for Arrow Strikers

The physical realities of the Old Testament foreshadow spiritual realities for people today, including you and me. Like a great novel, God's story of humanity uses Old Testament accounts to paint a picture of how we should live in this modern era.

In 2 Kings 13, Jehoash's actions during the physical battle directly correlate to our actions in the spiritual battle of life today. God wanted to use Jehoash to give Israel a victory, and He chose to use the physical act of Jehoash striking his arrows on the ground to do so. Every arrow strike resulted in a battle victory for the nation.

Still today, God wants to see victory for His kingdom. He doesn't have to work through people to fulfill His desires. He could supernaturally work on His own accord to accomplish His mission, and yet He chooses to use people to fulfill His plan. Yes, that means God wants to use *you* to accomplish His purposes. He wants to see the kingdom of God get victory after victory, and that can happen through your daily actions.

> *An arrow striker gives a wholehearted effort toward fulfilling God's purposes every moment possible.*

Every time we allow God to use us, we're figuratively striking our arrows. Whether it be an encouraging word, an act of kindness, or a specific opportunity, these occasions allow us to live every moment of every day to help advance God's purposes on Earth. In doing so, our daily actions to give, help, and serve others will lead to spiritual victories for eternity.

An arrow striker gives a wholehearted effort toward fulfilling

11

God's purposes every moment possible. God is looking for arrow strikers who'll commit to pursuing spiritual victories every single day. He wants you to maximize your life for Him by regularly striking your arrows.

God has a plan to fulfill through you. He has a work that must be done. He's looking for people to rise up, strike their arrows whenever possible, and give an all-out effort for Him. If you allow Him to, God will take your ordinary daily actions and produce extraordinary victories for His kingdom.

It's Your Turn

The battles you face daily may not be physical or involve warring nations, but we all share the common mission of building God's kingdom and fulfilling His purposes. There's no more important mission, and God wants to prepare you for your role in His plan. He wants to equip and empower you to step into all He has for you on any given day.

God has uniquely created every person with an innate, hardwired desire to make a difference. When most people sincerely investigate their deepest desires, they'll acknowledge an inner longing for their lives and actions to matter. And yet sometimes life's circumstances hinder our ability to give a wholehearted effort toward making a difference.

At times, people feel an internal tension regarding God's direction. They might sense God has ways He wants to use them, but they feel unqualified. Maybe they've failed too often. Maybe they're in the wrong career. Maybe they feel too young or too old. Maybe "life has gotten in the way," and other matters have taken precedence. Still others might wonder if they're doing the "right" things, and they question the success of their endeavors.

If you can relate to those thought patterns, it's okay. However, that's not where God wants you to stay. God wants to help you step into specific and unique opportunities every single day to help others, serve others, give to others, and encourage others. He has an exclusive daily plan for anyone who's willing to raise their hand and say, "God, I believe You can use even me."

In reality, your life has significance no matter your career, stage of life, spiritual maturity, or past failures. As long as you have breath, you play a part in God's plan for humanity. He'll give you countless opportunities to strike your arrows. It could be as big as helping someone follow Jesus, or it could be as little as an act of kindness toward a child. It might mean giving someone hope and encouragement, or it might look like simply being at the right place at the right time.

Everyone has these opportunities. How will you use these moments for good? The only thing that matters in the end is our service and obedience to God. As we live out God's purpose for our lives, we'll find He has something unique He wants to do each day to fulfill His overarching purposes.

As you read the pages of this book, I pray you discover ways to step into all God has for your life each day, even when you don't feel like you have much to offer. Your everyday decisions, actions, and words can affect your life, the lives of those around you, and ultimately, the kingdom of God.

Throughout this book, you'll see many examples of arrow strikers who used their everyday lives to amplify their influence and impact. We'll look at a passionate college freshman, a stay-at-home mom, a typical married couple, and many other everyday people who chose to be extraordinary. Some of the examples may feel daunting to you, and not something you'll ever do. Others may feel inconsequential or insignificant, and you could do way more. My purpose in sharing these examples is not for you to compare your present life to that of others, but to help you see potential ways you can make an even bigger difference without having to drastically change your life.

The examples of others shared throughout this book will give ideas of how you could more frequently strike your arrows—in ways you otherwise might not have realized. May they inspire you to tap into your God-given potential to make a difference daily without radically changing your way of living. The truth is, you can easily multiply your influence and leverage opportunities to impact others right now. May you be inspired to serve your role in God's plan and to recognize the opportunities He puts in front of you.

Following God and faithfully fulfilling His daily mission is not a one-size-fits-all approach. The goal of this book is to help you stay focused on His unique purposes for you, to faithfully step into those opportunities you encounter daily, and to give a wholehearted effort toward making a difference. You *can* make a substantial difference, more than you realize. He wants you to have a meaningful impact even on ordinary days. God will use you in your present stage of life and in your present career. He wants to use you just as you are.

God is looking for people to rise up every day and strike their arrows. He has purposes He wants to accomplish all the time, and He has chosen you to play an integral role in those purposes.

When you enthusiastically step into all God wants for your life, He'll do amazing things through you. And you'll have confidence that you're fulfilling His plan and the unique opportunities given to you. Someday when you stand before God, you'll know you gave your all and held nothing back.

CHAPTER 3

INFINITE POSSIBILITIES

I love seeing God's handiwork in nature. I often marvel at the beauty of His creation when I go to the mountains. There's just nothing like sitting on top of a Colorado "fourteener" (a 14,000-foot peak) with the warm sun beating down, while watching clouds float by at eye level. Seeing stunning views in every direction of peak after peak for miles on end is simply remarkable.

There's also a marvelous beauty about the beach. Looking out at the ocean with no land in the distant horizon is a spectacular sight. The calming ocean breeze and the rhythm of the waves is purely phenomenal. How did God come up with such an amazing creation?

Fortunately, you don't have to go on vacation to see God's amazing handiwork. In reality, God puts His marvelous creation on display everywhere we go, every single day. Whether it's a starry night or a beautiful landscape, people all over the world can stand in awe of His ingenuity.

But more than that, have you ever noted God's creativity in designing humanity? It's easy to take for granted the beauty in people you see every day at home or work or school. Did you know that every human has approximately three billion unique pairs of DNA in twenty-three chromosomes?[8] No one person is the same as another, despite billions of people being born over the millennia.

Every person in the world is divinely inspired, miraculously created, and uniquely gifted. That includes the poorest individuals in underdeveloped countries and the wealthiest individuals in Western nations. And yes, that even includes you. This means *you* are a work of art.

The apostle Paul articulated this in such a powerful way. When describing our desperate condition apart from Christ in the opening verses of Ephesians 2, he then contrasts God's work of grace through Christ and describes God's divine creativity:

> For we are God's masterpiece. He has created us anew in Christ Jesus, so we can do the good things he planned for us long ago.[9]

> *You were made for this very moment—to strike your arrows as opportunities arise.*

We're works of art, not because we're inherently beautiful or good, but because the Spirit of God lives in us. The Creator of this world has not only given us salvation but has also uniquely gifted us to fulfill His purposes. He has created *you* for this exact time in history, knowing everything that's happening in our world. You were made for this very moment—to strike your arrows as opportunities arise.

The divine Creator has uniquely created you for such a time as this. The dreams God has placed in your heart and the ideas He has given you exist because He loves you so much that He wants to use you to fulfill His purposes. As we marvel in His creative plan and develop the gifts He entrusts to us, amazing possibilities open up. Those "good things" God planned for you to accomplish long ago can become a reality today.

Gifting Back Our Gifts

God showers people with gifts all the time. It's like Christmas all year round. The only difference is that these are not material gifts for our consumption. Rather, they're intangible gifts for us to dispense. Have you ever heard the saying, "We're blessed to be a blessing"? God blesses you so you can be a blessing to other people. He gives us talents, skills, abilities, resources, and opportunities—for the benefit of others, not just for ourselves. Our gifts *from* God are to be given back *to* God. It's counterintuitive, right?

The Bible lists different spiritual gifts endowed to believers, and God distinctively provides these gifts to build up the body of Christ. Gifts of knowledge, discernment, healing, teaching, generosity, serving, encouragement, and administration are just some of the many examples explicitly revealed in Scripture.[10]

Did you know God also gives us "natural" gifts that He desires to use for His purposes? These are the skills and talents we naturally gravitate toward from our early adolescence, and they develop as the years progress. We might not think of them as spiritual gifts, and yet God gives us these abilities so we can use them to accomplish what He wants to do through our lives.

A man named Bezalel, a contemporary of Moses, had many God-ordained natural skills that allowed him to oversee the development of the tabernacle. The Lord describes this man's skillset in these words:

> I have filled him with the Spirit of God, with ability and intelligence, with knowledge and all craftsmanship, to devise artistic designs, to work in gold, silver, and bronze, in cutting stones for setting, and in carving wood, to work in every craft.[11]

Bezalel was an artist—a creative individual with an irreplaceable skill set. No other person had his exact combination of skills, wisdom, intellect, and ability. God specifically intended to use the skill of his hands to accomplish what needed done at that moment in history.

In reality, the natural gifts that develop within us can be used for supernatural purposes. What skills, talents, and abilities do you have? Are there new ways you can use those gifts to serve the church, your community, or people in need? The possibilities of your impact are truly endless as you tap into these gifts—as you strike your arrows.

Sometimes God also gifts people with opportunities. We often think of these as being in the right place at the right time. And yet when it comes to serving God, happenstance and coincidence are always His divine providence.

Opportunities that occur on any normal, mundane day are actually a gift from God to be a blessing to others. When arrow strikers positively respond to those gifted opportunities, they're giving that opportunity back to God, allowing Him to work through the situation at hand. God will take your surrendered opportunity and accomplish His will in that single moment.

A few years ago, I received a mailer to help support a missions organization having a positive impact in another country for God's kingdom. Upon opening the mail, however, I did what people often do. I threw it in the trash. I had little financial margin at the time, so I elected to pass on the opportunity. As I walked away from the trash can, I felt God nudge me. This prompted an internal conversation with myself on whether I should send that organization a whopping ten dollars. Can you believe that? I know—I'm embarrassed to admit it.

Now, not everyone has the cashflow to give an extra ten dollars toward a cause, but I did, and yet I almost missed an opportunity to play my part in making an eternal difference through that small act of generosity. After heeding God's convincing nudge, I went back to the trash can, pulled out the envelope, and mailed my small contribution to that organization. I almost lost that opportunity, but I'm thankful God graciously nudged me to give that opportunity back to Him so He could multiply my small donation for His greater purposes.

People everywhere have opportunities like this on a regular basis. Every moment is an opportunity to act—an opportunity to strike our arrows. What we do in those moments is our choice.

God desires that you take the opportunities He gives and surrender them back to Him so He can work supernaturally through you to accomplish His will. Who knows what could happen when you give your gifts, talents, abilities, resources, and opportunities back to God? You just never know what a single arrow strike might accomplish in God's divine master plan, but it'll be amazing.

Your "Eventually"

I was twenty-five years old when the idea for this book first developed. I'd begun working as an associate pastor at James River Church in Springfield, Missouri. While I occasionally jotted down ideas and concepts for the book, the timing didn't feel right to actually develop it, and I put writing on the shelf.

In the years that followed, I frequently talked to my family and friends about my sense from God that I was to write this book. I always said "eventually" to writing, but I took no action until the summer of 2019. God had given me multiple clear promptings in prayer regarding His desire for me to write, so I finally stepped into the process.

After fifteen years since inception, the book you're now reading was published. God had a specific task He wanted me to complete. My "eventually" approach almost caused me to miss an opportunity to strike my arrows. Fortunately, we serve a loving God who patiently guides us with consistent promptings to follow His lead.

Have you ever sensed that God specifically orchestrated something for you to step into? The intersection of your giftings and opportunities may have caused you to realize how God has an exclusive plan designed specifically for you. Maybe you've wondered if you should volunteer at school, help a ministry, share your story, give financially, or write a book (like me). You can fill in the blank for you.

Do you have an "eventually" in your life? Is there something you sense that God has prompted you to do but you maybe haven't acted on it yet?

Following God's leading involves action on our part, and that might mean you have to put in the effort. As Thomas Edison said, "Opportunity is missed by most people because it is dressed in overalls and looks like work."[12]

Sometimes people underestimate the impact they can have. They downplay their gifts, abilities, and resources. They might compare themselves to others and feel as though they have little to offer. Some even allow distractions, busyness, and the cares of life to take greater precedence, and they chalk up their inaction to the "eventually" mentality. But God wants more than that. He has a purpose for you right here, today. And He'll equip you to fulfill His leading in your life.

God births ideas within people because He actually wants to use them as part of His overarching agenda. So when God gives you a prompting, a calling, or a sense of purpose, He usually wants you to step into that leading immediately (not eventually).

In reality, the grass isn't always greener somewhere else or at another time. The opportunities elsewhere or later aren't usually bigger. The timing doesn't normally improve. If you're waiting for perfect conditions, you'll likely never have them. Pastor Mark Batterson puts it this way:

> You'll never have enough. You'll never be enough.
> You'll never do enough. But don't let that keep you
> from giving what you have, being who you are, and
> doing what you can. Don't let what you cannot do
> keep you from doing what you can.[13]

God wants you to move forward in your present situation despite imperfect scenarios. He has special ways He'd like to work through you right away. Circumstances need not be perfect to maximize a moment to the best of your ability. God simply wants you to strike your arrows and give your best so He can produce a spiritual victory.

The Legacy of J. R. R. Tolkien

J. R. R. Tolkien was an accomplished creative. His most notable work, *The Lord of the Rings* trilogy, has sold more than 150,000,000 copies and is listed as the ninth bestselling book of all time.[14] The movies based on his trilogy have grossed more than $2.9 billion in revenue.[15] *Forbes* magazine ranked Tolkien fifth on a recent list of the highest income over the past twelve months for deceased celebrities.[16] That's quite an impressive record.

However, I would say his book sales and gross revenue were not his greatest legacy. As incredible as those achievements were, I suggest that his greatest impact was his influence on other people. Tolkien used his gift of writing to connect with other individuals, including C. S. Lewis, whom he helped lead to Christ.[17] Millions have been influenced through Lewis's ministry, which has helped lead countless numbers of people to Christ.

Think about this for a moment. What if Tolkien never reached out to Lewis? What if he didn't show the love of Christ to him? What if he didn't engage in conversation and share the gospel message with him? That means millions of people may not have experienced the impact they received through books like

Mere Christianity and other popular writings that God guided Lewis to create.

This is like what happened with Andrew and his brother Simon (later called Peter) in the Bible. When Andrew first heard Jesus speak, he was greatly affected. Did he keep this newfound relationship to himself? Not at all. He went to his brother and told him he needed to meet Jesus.[18] Andrew introduced Simon Peter to Jesus, and the rest is history. We all know Jesus's profound reference to Peter when He said, "On this rock I will build my church."[19] After Jesus's ascension to heaven, Peter became the leader of the early church.

Have you ever considered what would have happened if Andrew hadn't told Peter about Jesus? Who would have led the church? How would things have transpired? Fortunately, God had it all figured out, and Andrew's prompting to share the news about Jesus played an integral role in the formation of the early church.

What does this mean for us today? You never know the impact that one conversation, one introduction, or one act of kindness can have on an individual—or all the people *that* individual might eventually influence.

This is what happens when you remain faithful to the purposes God has for you in your environment—in your family, church, workplace, neighborhood, school, and community.

What would happen if you read a Bible story to your kids every night of the week? What miracles might you see if you prayed with your spouse each day? What if God wanted you to write one note of encouragement per week to a family member? What if God asked you to give financially to a local charity?

What if God asked you to pray an extra fifteen minutes each day for your teachers, school officials, and leaders in government? What if you shared your journey of following Christ with your neighbor, friend, or co-worker?

This list of how you can strike your arrows has infinite possibilities. Just think of what God could do through you in small acts of kindness, ordinary conversations, or simple steps of faith. You just never know what might happen when you make God's purposes a priority, then take small steps forward while believing your actions *will* make a difference.

CHAPTER 4

AN EYE FOR OPPORTUNITY

In 1994, after learning about the prospects of the Internet's capabilities, Jeff Bezos listed twenty products he thought consumers might buy online.

> He narrowed the list to what he felt were the five most promising products, which included compact discs, computer hardware, computer software, videos, and books. Bezos finally decided that his new business would sell books online, because of the large worldwide demand for literature, the low unit price for books, and the huge number of titles available in print.[20]

When Jeff Bezos launched an online bookstore out of his garage in July 1995, no one (including Bezos) knew how that decision would someday affect the world. People quickly learned of Amazon.com, and the online bookstore experienced explosive growth immediately. As the years went by, Amazon had opportunity after opportunity to expand its offerings.

From a business perspective, each opportunity represented potential growth for the company, and that led to its dominant position as the largest ecommerce company in the world. When the Covid-19 pandemic arrived in early 2020, Amazon was positioned for its biggest opportunity as businesses all over the world shut down. People turned online more than ever before for their shopping needs, and Amazon seized that momentum. After an unprecedented year, Amazon reported a nearly 200 percent increase in profits.[21]

Amazon began the movement that forever changed the way people shop, and it all started with Bezos responding to and capitalizing on each opportunity he saw available.

But this experience doesn't apply only to the marketplace. In reality, every person or organization has a window of opportunity to make an impact throughout life. Every week you can express life-giving words and deeds that could powerfully affect another individual.

I wonder what went through King Jehoash's mind when Elisha told him to strike the arrows against the ground. No doubt he likely thought, *Say what? Elisha, are you serious? That's absurd.* I suppose many of us probably would respond in a similar manner. Maybe he felt silly striking a handful of arrows against the ground. Or maybe his weak faith got the best of him, and he didn't really believe his actions could have such an impact. Or maybe he didn't think the actual act of striking had any significant meaning.

Scripture tells us that his three arrow strikes gave Israel three battle victories over Aram.[22] Considering what Israel was up against in the years preceding this moment, that would have been a phenomenal end result. One might think Elisha would be satisfied with such a result. But his frustration and disappointment were evident.

The reason?

God simply had more in mind for Israel than three battle victories. Elisha saw the larger opportunity, but Jehoash missed it.

We can only speculate why Jehoash missed the opportunity to give Israel an even greater

> God has a unique plan and purpose for people every day.

victory, but there's an important lesson for believers. God has a unique plan and purpose for people every day. Regardless of what He asks us to do, our faith-filled response to God's leading determines the extent of God's favor, provision, and blessing in our lives. Our anticipation of God's working leads to extraordinary spiritual victories.

More Than Fire Insurance

God honors our obedient steps of faith, beginning with our faith in Christ. However, salvation is a new birth—a beginning, not an end result. Salvation is more than just fire insurance, helping us escape the flames of hell. God's gift of salvation is only the beginning of the abundant life He wants us to live.

Jesus shared this concept with His disciples. He said, "Freely you have received, freely give."[23] God didn't give the gift of salvation for us to keep to ourselves. Rather, He wants us to share with others the unconditional love He has given us. He wants people everywhere to experience His abundant life-giving power.

That's part of His redemptive master plan. God not only wants us to know Him; He also wants us to make Him known.

In our individualistic Western culture, it's easy to focus on *our* salvation. It's sometimes more difficult to embrace how God wants us to live out that salvation through our words, deeds, and actions. Let's always remember this: The assurance of heaven is a true comfort throughout our lifetimes, yet as believers who better understand what God has done for us, we can find no shortage of motivation for living *all* our lives in His service. Every day of this life (and not just the eternal life that awaits us) is an incredible blessing *now*. God wants to use people—including you—to make a difference here and now.

You have a profound opportunity now to maximize your eternal impact beyond just making it to heaven. God has purposed for you to help others find and follow Him. He has gifted you with an abundance of skills, talents, abilities, resources, and opportunities to reach others.

But how do we know which opportunities to take?

Developing an eye for opportunity is key to a person's growth and increased influence on others. Not all opportunities merit our focus and attention, but wisdom and experience will help a person recognize and embrace the right opportunities.

As you maintain a sacrificially obedient heart to God's directives in your life, you'll find greater discernment in how God wants you to daily live out your faith.

Just Two Coins

Do you remember when people brought in their offerings as Jesus hung out with the disciples in the temple? The Bible says He "sat down opposite the place where the offerings were put and watched the crowd putting their money into the temple treasury. Many rich people threw in large amounts."[24]

As people dropped off their money into the temple receptacles, no doubt there were onlookers who noticed the substantial sizes of many offerings. You can imagine their thoughts as they sized up the contributions. Much could be done with those big offerings. I'm guessing some bystanders were simply noting how good business had been for the rich folks.

Then a poor widow came to drop off her offering. It was not significant. She had just two small copper coins, probably worth only a few cents.[25] Clink. Clink. That was it.

Most people would look at that and see an insignificant impact. Two coins, as shiny and polished as they may have been, were nothing compared to all the money others were putting in. Did she wonder if those two coins would make any difference?

The actual act of giving two small coins meant little for the temple. It was a very insignificant amount of money and not much could happen, practically speaking, with just two coins. Yet Jesus pointed out that the widow's sacrificial act was vastly significant: "This poor widow has put more into the treasury than all the others. They all gave out of their wealth; but she, out of her poverty, put in everything—all she had to live on."[26]

That seems counterintuitive, right?

Two coins were nothing compared to the hundreds of coins

given by the wealthy people. It's obvious from a mathematical perspective, but God's math equations don't always match up to our human perspective. God does impossible math.

Why did Jesus say her gift was worth more?

This woman was all in. She sacrificed what she had. She was willing to risk everything—to give everything to God. She was an arrow striker.

At the end of the day, it's not just about what people do for God. What we do is no doubt important, but when you boil it down, it's not so much our actual actions that matter. Rather, obedience to God is the ultimate indicator of your heart and desires.

We know salvation and life with God for eternity are freely given to anyone who puts their faith in Christ. Period. Our works don't save us.[27] The Bible makes the way of salvation ultra-clear. "If you openly declare that Jesus is Lord and believe in your heart that God raised him from the dead, you will be saved."[28] You don't have to hit a certain threshold in your giving. You don't have to introduce a certain number of people to Jesus. You don't have to do so many acts of kindness. Those aren't the measurables God looks at. He looks at your heart. He looks at your sacrifice and surrender. He looks at your obedience.

Did you obey God? Did you do what God asked you to do? Did you remain faithful to His calling and purposes for your life? Did you use your gifts to your maximum potential? Did you spend your time, energy, and money on what matters most? These are the questions that matter in the end.

Say Yes

Leanne was a single mom in her mid-forties when she had a special opportunity to impact others. Over the years she'd relied on family, friends, and local community organizations to help her make ends meet. She never wanted to rely on the help from others, financially and otherwise, but her station in life and financial circumstances didn't afford her the privilege of self-sufficiency. Then she found a stable job with a solid income that helped provide for her needs. This positioned her for a powerful moment to give back what she'd so often received.

While many people faced dire circumstances resulting from the Covid-19 pandemic, Leanne was fortunate to remain financially secure. She had the advantage of remaining employed at a safe job, and she continued to pay all her bills despite the turbulent times.

On one particular day, Leanne received a $500 bonus check from her employer. As any single mom would tell you, this was a massive blessing to her, especially during a global pandemic. In that moment, Leanne had a choice. What would she do with this money? How would she spend it? She could keep it all to herself, and frankly, she deserved it. But that's not what she did.

Leanne saw an opportunity. Her eyes were attuned to the moment, and she knew exactly what she wanted to do with that bonus. Since she'd received so much financial help in years past, she wanted to give back. Leanne chose to give the entire bonus to the same local organization that had previously helped her. That way, new families facing economic hardship could experience the same generosity she once received.

This brought Leanne full circle. She was blessed so that she could be a blessing to others in need. That community service organization used her $500 to help ten different families. How amazing!

People often think of God's personal will for their lives as some magical and singular pathway that God has designed for each person. While God does have certain desires for people, this doesn't mean He has one singular will for each person's life—which if you don't discover, you're out of luck. Fortunately, that's not how God works.

Understanding God's will for us doesn't have to be complicated. God makes His will known to us every day as He gives us opportunities to step into what He reveals to us. We simply need to keep our eyes and ears attuned to His leading. As we spend time with Him, our sensitivity to hear from Him grows, and our awareness of His leading becomes clearer.

But what if you're not sure if an opportunity is from God? That's where faith comes into play.

When our lifestyle is aligned with what we know God reveals in Scripture, following God's will is fairly easy. God often gives us the choice to make certain decisions and to step into opportunities that don't run contrary to His Word.

God's will is not some far-fetched, grandiose plan you have to discover. The ordinary opportunities you experience every day will frequently reveal God's will for you in that moment. Like Leanne, you have a choice to say yes to those opportunities. Opportunity is everywhere, and God has plenty of things He'd like to do through you, even when you least expect it.

Our spiritual life is not *just* about our deeds, but it also includes our deeds. That's why James noted that "faith without deeds is dead."[29] Our faith in God is ultimately expressed *through* our deeds. Your faith expresses itself through various daily actions to help, serve, give, and share with one another. Striking your arrows is how you display your faith.

Your daily deeds determine your destiny. They determine the outcome of the situations you face every day. And what you do today leads to future opportunities tomorrow.

The key is simply to say yes. Say yes to what is in front of you. Say yes to what God reveals in Scripture. Say yes to sacrificial giving, serving, sharing, and encouraging.

> *Striking your arrows is how you display your faith.*

As the apostle Paul said, "Whatever you do, whether in word or deed, do it all in the name of the Lord Jesus, giving thanks to God the Father through him."[30] When you do, you're doing God's will.

Have you said yes to the opportunities you've been given lately? Do you live with an understanding of how God wants to work as you faithfully commit to His will each day? The sacrifice may be great, but the reward is always greater when you step into God's daily destiny.

CHAPTER 5

THE CLOCK IS TICKING,
BUT GOD IS THE TIMEKEEPER

Her name was Rachel Schultz. She'd married the love of her life, and a dozen years later she had four small children, from infant to age eleven. Then the unthinkable happened. In January 1943, her husband, Bill—in his early thirties—died of heart disease. She now had to care for their four children on her own. However, that wasn't the end of her tragic story.

Only two years later, in March 1945, Rachel's second-born son, Dick, was struck and killed by an oncoming train while playing with friends on a railroad bridge. Rachel's agony and painful suffering were further amplified.

Times were tumultuous for Rachel, but she had to figure out how to move forward despite such horrific circumstances. Left with her three children—Donna, Mary, and Clifford—she had a choice to make. One option was to move from her current home to the town of LeMars, Iowa, where she'd have support from extended family. Another option was to move thirty miles farther south to Sioux City, Iowa, and take a teaching position with the public school system. Both options had pros and cons. LeMars would be far more comfortable with family around, and her family lobbied her to choose this option. But Rachel couldn't shake an inner sense that God wanted her to move to Sioux City instead. So that's what she did.

Rachel bought a little white house across an alley from First Assembly, a thriving church in that community. Her children immediately jumped into the church's activities upon moving there.

By the time her oldest, Donna, graduated from high school, she'd become close friends with four Hardy girls. It just so happened the girls had an older brother who'd just returned from the Navy. Bud Hardy set his eyes on the beautiful Donna Schultz. And the rest, as they say, is history.

Rachel was my great-grandmother (you might have guessed there was some connection). Her decision to move to Sioux City, Iowa, after those two tragedies charted the course for her daughter to meet my Grandpa Hardy. Their involvement in that church put our family on a course that led my dad into full-time vocational ministry. His life and leadership in my life resulted in my attending a Bible college where I met my wife, Ashley. And now we're raising our three kids to be the next generation of committed followers of Jesus.

This Christ-centered multi-generation family was the result of an "ordinary" decision to find a job. Rachel didn't set out to change history with her decision to take a teaching position. She simply needed to provide for her family after such tragedies, and taking that job was the step God wanted her to take in that moment.

Some would say, "Aw, it's just a move to a place with a job." But as you can see, there was a whole lot more involved than just providing for her children. God had a bigger purpose in mind. The future generations in her lineage would forever be impacted. Her decisions and actions mattered, and they changed the trajectory for the generations that followed.

Like Rachel, the decisions we face on a regular basis provide opportunities for us to strike our arrows. Often these decisions are made to satisfy the immediate need. And yet the decisions we make and the opportunities we face have the potential to produce a significant outcome far greater than simply meeting the immediate need.

Life Is Short

"This is the first day of the rest of your life." "Live each day as if it's your last." "Life is short."

Popular phrases like these are designed to motivate people to maximize their days on Earth. Most people understand the reality of finite time, but their perceptions of it—and their response to the reality—will differ for each person. Some travel the world. Others buy all the toys and gadgets they want. They know they have limited time to enjoy their life, so they want to capitalize on the pleasures of the moment.

When I became a father, I can't tell you how often people told me to enjoy time with my kids because it would go by fast. They described how one day you blink and they're graduating from high school or getting married. Almost every empty-nester I talked to said something along those lines, which only confirmed to me that life is short. Time does go by fast, so we need to make the most of our time with loved ones.

What about life spiritually speaking?

Do you live with an eternal focus in mind, knowing that life on Earth is short? Do you spend your days wisely, knowing any day here could be your last?

God gives every person a finite amount of time on Earth. The amount is different for every individual, but every person's life has a timer that's ticking down. If our responsibility as believers is to steward the time given to us, we ought to use every moment possible to make a difference for the Lord. We must look for and step into God's leading each day, because we don't know what tomorrow will hold.

In the Bible, James echoed this reality: "How do you know what your life will be like tomorrow? Your life is like the morning fog—it's here a little while, then it's gone."[31]

While many people look at their limited time on Earth with fear and anxiety, that's not God's desire. He wants you to look at this life knowing you have a small window to make a difference in the lives of others. That's how He set up our entire human existence. It was the first "limited time opportunity" ever created.

With your time limited as eternity quickly approaches, God wants you to understand the unique opportunity you have to reach people, serve others, and fulfill His plan for your life every single day. That's why the apostle Paul told believers to "make the most of every opportunity."[32]

Everyone has the same amount of time—168 hours per week.

How we use that time is up to us. No matter how much longer we have left in this life, let's embrace opportunities to make a difference each day—and watch God do amazing things through us.

Exponential Spiritual Effect

The decisions you make and the opportunities you take matter to God and to others around you. And many of these choices and actions will have an eternal impact. Sometimes people misunderstand the significance of the moment because it's hard to look through the lens of eternity.

> *Sometimes people misunderstand the significance of the moment because it's hard to look through the lens of eternity.*

Let's face it. We don't have eyes to see the unseen realm, at least not yet. As believers, someday we'll have a clearer eternal perspective, but right now we see only with our natural eyes, as we perceive what's physically in front of us. Since we don't think like God thinks, it's impossible to fully comprehend His ways. The Bible even acknowledges that our thoughts and God's thoughts are different.[33]

Why the difference?

Because He has eternal eyes, while we have natural eyes. This has huge implications. When we look at our lives day to day through our natural eyes, heaven seems super far away. Have you noticed that? It feels as if heaven is another lifetime away.

We often think eternity starts when Jesus comes back, or we think it begins when we pass away. But eternity is here. Yes, everyone is living in eternity right now. Granted, it's just the first part of eternity. For believers, it's the part *before* we find ourselves living in a perfect and sinless world. But it's still part of eternity. Eternity existed before we were born, and it infinitely continues beyond our human comprehension.

Why is this important?

If we live our daily lives with the sense that eternity is a long time from now, we might live with a lesser sense of urgency to make a difference in the present. The more time we think we have until we stand before God, the less significant each moment seems for God's eternal purposes.

But that couldn't be further from the truth.

Your everyday opportunities to make a difference do matter *today*. Each present moment is just as important now as it will be twenty, forty, or sixty years from now. In fact, the importance of your actions is actually greater now than it will be later, because of the "exponential spiritual effect."

The exponential spiritual effect is the cumulative influence your actions have over the course of your life, starting today. The exponential spiritual effect works in the same way that a stock or mutual fund has the potential to exponentially grow over time (and the more time you have, the greater potential for growth you have).

The more times you strike your arrows and make a difference in the lives of others, the more likely it is that those you've influenced will in turn influence others. And the exponential spiritual effect takes a snowball form that gets increasingly bigger as more and more people you've influenced will then live out their faith with purpose and intentionality.

Let me illustrate with a twentieth-century arrow striker who had a profound effect.

Mordecai Who?

Have you ever heard of Mordecai Ham? Most people haven't heard of him. But he had a major exponential spiritual effect, far greater than most people could probably ever imagine.

Mordecai Ham served God as an evangelist for most of his adult years. Week after week he traveled the United States holding services and tent revivals for dozens of people. With each event, a few people would give their life to Christ. Thanks to the exponential spiritual effect, each of them would go on to lead others to Jesus as well. That effect could be drawn back to Mordecai.

The beauty of arrow striking is that when the arrow is struck often enough, sometimes it hits big. On one cold November night in Charlotte, North Carolina, Ham spoke the same message he gave every night. He gave the same altar call he gave every night. But on that night, kneeling at the altar was a man named Billy Graham. Mordecai had the pleasure of leading to the Lord this man who would become a titan of the faith.[34] Thanks to that night, the exponential spiritual effect flew to tenfold returns and beyond, all because Mordecai Ham just kept striking his arrows.

The exponential spiritual effect often starts small. But when you continue faithfully in the small things, you eventually get to see explosive results. Just think of what life for the kingdom of God would have looked like if Mordecai Ham hadn't followed his assignment from God. What if he didn't speak at that tent meeting? What if he chose to do something different instead, because it was a small, seemingly inconsequential meeting in North Carolina?

That one meeting alone kicked off a massive impact that would literally change millions of lives for eternity. Did he know that effect going into the meeting that night? No way. But I do know he understood the significance of every single opportunity God placed before him, including the "regular" everyday opportunities. He faithfully embraced the moments in front of him, and God used him far beyond his imagination.

That's why, starting today, God wants you to live each day with purpose and intentionality, understanding the significance of every moment—in both big things and small things.

Your life matters to God, and your life matters to others. Maximizing the opportunities that come your way has the potential for huge implications. The fact is, you don't know what impact you might have on a person. Those who live unaware might miss out on what God wants to do through them to impact other people.

You might not be a superstar Christian, but that's not what God wants. He wants you—just as you are—to faithfully follow His lead and obey His directives as they come.

Think about it for a moment. Think of the various people who influenced you to follow God. What if those persons didn't share God's love with you, invite you to church, encourage you, or help you in a time of need? Have you ever wondered what life would be like for you if they hadn't done that?

You may never introduce a Billy Graham to Jesus, but your smile may be the very thing an elderly person in a nursing home may need to see. Your small act of kindness might speak louder than words to your unsaved co-worker. Your generosity to a single mom may be the perfect example she needs her kids to see. Your community involvement may allow you to influence the governing authorities. Your serving role in the local church can transform lives.

What we do each day has greater significance than we might realize. Striking our arrows will maximize the exponential spiritual effect God wants to have through our lives. In my case, if my Great-Grandma Schultz chose comfort instead of stepping into God's leading, I can assure you the book you're reading right now would not exist.

Be Up and Awake

When people begin to understand the potential significance of each day, a shift takes place in their thoughts and actions. They live with a sense of expectation and anticipation of what God will do. Since God might be up to something special, arrow strikers more readily look for doors of opportunity.

Jesus acknowledged this priority when He said, "As long as it is day, we must do the works of him who sent me. Night is coming, when no one can work."[35] He knew why He'd come, and He knew the significance of His moment in history, so He kept His focus on that purpose each day.

The apostle Paul also expressed this sense of passion, priority, and urgency in his letter to the Roman church:

> Make sure that you don't get so absorbed and ex-
> hausted in taking care of all your day-by-day obli-

gations that you lose track of the time and doze off, oblivious to God. The night is about over, dawn is about to break. Be up and awake to what God is doing![36]

Every day that goes by is one day closer to our being enjoined with Christ forever. This means there's no time like the present to make an impact on others.

The time is now.

This is your moment.

This is your opportunity.

You were created for this moment in history, and God has a plan He wants you to fulfill. He uniquely positioned you where you are for this season of life. God wants you to embrace the moment and recognize its significance and importance within His divine master plan.

Many various needs exist among your friends, family, co-workers, and neighbors. Some people might need encouragement. Some might need help in an area of life. Some might need a miracle. Some might need salvation. God may have sent you to be the one to provide hope and encouragement. Why? Because of His great love for people.

Do you see how important these moments can be for others?

I hope you'll begin living with a greater sense of passion, priority, and urgency every day, appreciating the significance of each moment and opportunity. As you strike your arrows from this point forward—in big things and small—be expectant because of God's great love, and watch Him use you in ways you never thought possible.

PART 2

LIVING LIFE

The Bible often likens the spiritual life to a race. We're running a spiritual race, and He wants to help you run to win. God wants you to go all out for Him. He wants your best.

He wants to be number one in your life. That happens when you give an all-out effort toward God. In doing so, you'll live the strong and fulfilling life He desires for you.

As people seek to give a full-on effort for God, sometimes obstacles get in the way. We might face difficulties that have the potential to steer us off track if we're not careful. But God has more for you, and this next section will show you how to ensure your motivation remains strong and resolute for God's intended purposes.

Over the next seven chapters, we'll look at seven specific traits of arrow strikers. These are characteristics, actions, and behaviors that maximize people's effectiveness in accomplishing God's purposes in their everyday lives. As people develop the healthy habits we examine, they'll confidently know they gave their all and held nothing back as they stepped into God's daily plan for their lives.

God wants you to live with joy and fulfillment. He has a lavish life designed just for you. As you continually commit your daily life to God, you'll experience the abundant life He desires for you, living a fully blessed life now and for eternity.

Download a study guide for personal reflection or group discussion: www.arrowstriker.com/guide

CHAPTER 6

FEAR LESS

James and Grace lived in Mississippi as a typical American family in the South. James served as the business administrator of a local church. Grace was a stay-at-home mom caring for their precious kids.

In 2014, they felt a stirring in their hearts. God had spoken to them about the next chapter He had for them, and this little stirring continued to grow. During this unsettled period, they wholeheartedly committed to surrender absolutely to God's leading, no matter what He requested.

Little did they know, His request would be huge and life-altering. Through prayer and counsel with others, they felt that God had called them to serve as missionaries to a sensitive area of North Africa.

Yikes! That wasn't on their radar at all.

It was the biggest step of faith they would ever take. Yet they couldn't shake the clear sense from God that this was their next step. They felt compelled to go, and they were excited to give their wholehearted commitment to fulfilling His plan.

Of course, they thought of every possible obstacle to overcome as they mentally prepared for this journey. They spoke only English. They had no money. They knew no one in that region except one missionary. And yet they were called to go, so God took care of those obstacles, including $70,000 in student debt that was miraculously forgiven.

After resigning from their church, they began the fundraising journey. They toured across the United States speaking in churches about the work they were preparing to do. Upon raising the necessary financial support, they departed in January 2019 to give their wholehearted effort to fulfill God's next assignment.

Can you imagine the emotions they felt as they boarded a one-way flight to Africa? No doubt they experienced fear and anxiety as they embarked on this life-altering decision. Fortunately, they also had confidence in God's leading.

Within the first year of their missionary journey, they began building relationships with people and made several new friends. Nearly every new friend had never even met a Christian, let alone heard of Jesus. As James and Grace shared the good news of Jesus, many of these people experienced who God is for the first time. All this was because James and Grace had boarded that one-way flight, knowing God wanted others to find and follow Him. What an inspiring family of arrow strikers!

Take a Deep Breath

You're probably not called to North Africa like James and Grace. In fact, most people are not called overseas to be a missionary. Going to any foreign land can be a fearful thing. In reality, most people prefer the safety and comfort of their present lives here. The thought of doing something out of their comfort zones is a daunting thought. It's downright scary.

Now, hopefully your blood pressure and anxiety levels are not rising as you read these words. You don't have to fear the thought of leaving all you've ever known to go to a distant land. Instead, I have good news for you. The opportunities and purposes God has for you are actually right in front of you. God wants to use you today, right where you are.

Did you know everyone is "in ministry"? Your marriage is part of your ministry. Your parenting is part of your ministry. Your career is part of your ministry. Your neighborhood is part of your ministry. Your school, church, and community involvement are part of your ministry. Every aspect of your life presents opportunities to step into what God has for you. This is God's calling for all of us.

People often fear surrendering everything to God because they don't want the potential of a major "calling" God may give them. People might fear that God will ask them to move to an undesirable location or do something crazy if they surrender every part of their life to Him. So they don't quite surrender fully to God's purposes. And yet God wants all of you. He wants "all your heart."[37]

In the end, following God's directives is what matters most. God seeks a wholehearted commitment so we can know Him, serve one another, and step into what He has for us. That's our greatest responsibility in the grand scheme of eternity.

Why Do We Fear?

God knew fear was a real struggle for humanity, which is why He often told people throughout the Bible to not be afraid. In fact, the most frequent command in Scripture is "Do not fear."

Fear sometimes hinders our ability to walk in the purposes of God. It's the very thing that keeps us from the courage and design He has for our lives. Fear slows some people from acting immediately when they sense God's leading. For others, it literally cripples them from moving forward. Why is that?

A few reasons come to mind. First, if people had a bad experience in the past, and circumstances didn't pan out as they thought they would, they might not want to go through that kind of pain again. These feelings of fear and anxiety creep in, crippling their ability to embrace God-given opportunities.

Some people even have scars from the past, possibly from their upbringing, and they don't want to relive those moments. Even if done unconsciously, they don't want to open up an unhealed wound. Rather than dealing with the past and healing their wounds, this fear forfeits their ability to step into certain God-ordained moments.

Probably the biggest fear many people have relates to perceptions by others. We tend to fear what others will think of us. But when believers live out their faith by committing acts of kindness, helping others, and doing what God asks them to do, these actions show unsaved family members, neighbors, and co-workers where they really stand in their faith.

The fears of what others will think sometimes relates to their perception of our status. Occasionally God asks us to do something that's "below" our qualifications, and we fear that people might look down on us.

This reminds me of my friend John Higginbotham, a true arrow striker. As a successful businessman, John had run several businesses that generated annual revenue in the millions of dollars, and he was clearly living the American dream. In 2008, he sold his successful business but remained an employee there until 2014. After that, he had his hands in miscellaneous business ventures to make ends meet while he began a journey of asking God what step to take next.

Over the years, John had a heart for the homeless, and he frequently supported charitable organizations financially and by volunteering his time. On one distinctive night in the summer of 2014, he had a "God dream" where an idea was birthed on how to help the homeless in a whole new way. However, he kept it silent. He ignored it. He even tried to run from it, but he couldn't shake the clear sense that God had spoken to him.

Eventually he shared this dream with others, and God used those conversations to amplify his passion for the homeless. He started speaking with many folks out on the streets, trying to get a better understanding of their needs and how he could help.

After much prayer and reflection, he sensed God asking him to do something outside the box. He had a plan and vision to help homeless people across the United States. He developed a list of supplies every homeless person would need but which together had to fit inside a five-gallon bucket—so they could easily be transported and protected from inclement weather. Plus, he knew the bucket could double as a seat.

As he shared this concept with others, the idea immediately

resonated with people. This confirmed that he was on the right track, and in 2018 John officially launched the new ministry called God's Bucket Brigade.

In the first year alone, God's Bucket Brigade gave away five hundred buckets to homeless individuals. One recipient was a girl named Trish. She was living in the woods with her dog—starving, freezing, and terrified while running from a horrible situation. Little did John know his fearless obedience would transform her life. She later wrote this to him:

> You and your organization saved me and my dog's life... Thank you from the bottom of my heart. We are currently in our own apartment, I have a stable job, and am healing more and more each day.

John had every right to fear what people might think. Here this businessman had given up a successful career path to help homeless people. And yet John knew what was most important. John's confidence in God helped him strike his arrows, and Trish is just one of countless individuals who've benefited from his courageous submission.

You're in Good Company

Have you ever let fear stop you from doing something you felt like you were supposed to do? I know I have.

Maybe God asked you to share the gospel with a stranger, but you feared what they would think. Or maybe you were to invite a friend to church, but you didn't want to lose the friendship. Or maybe you feared running out of money if you gave to an organization. Or maybe you didn't want your comfort taken away.

God might ask us to do a variety of things as we serve Him, but He also equips us with the tools we need to accomplish those things. If you fear how God may lead you in a given situation, know that He'll give you the confidence and courage you desire so you can rise to the occasion. God always honors our brave obedience and fearless surrender to Him.

Many heroes of the faith experienced fear, including Jacob, Moses, Joshua, and David, just to name a few. Even the apostle Paul asked for prayer that he might fearlessly make known the mystery of the gospel. He faced fear as he tried to reach people and make an impact for the kingdom.[38]

Perhaps this is why throughout Scripture we see God instruct His people to be strong and courageous. This can be a meaningful source of inspiration for us. I love how God specifically encouraged Joshua: "Be strong and courageous. Do not be afraid; do not be discouraged, for the LORD your God will be with you wherever you go."[39] God's loving encouragement equips us with the strength we need to overcome fear and embrace God-given opportunities.

> God's loving encouragement equips us with the strength we need to overcome fear and embrace God-given opportunities.

Even the heroes of the faith made it through their fears, and they left an incredible legacy for us to follow. If you fear God asking you to step into an opportunity, rest assured. You're in good company.

Three Responses to Fear

Have you ever noticed how God-given opportunities are often accompanied by fear?

As soon as the door of opportunity opens, fear walks right through. In those moments, we have a choice. Will we allow fear to stop us from fulfilling God's assignment, or will we embrace the moment despite those feelings? When people experience fear in response to a God-given opportunity, they generally respond in one of three ways: flee, fight it, or face it.

Jonah is the classic example when we think of someone who fled out of fear. While trying to avoid the responsibilities God had for him in Nineveh, he escaped on a boat. It didn't take long for Jonah to realize God was right there with him, waiting for him to obey. Sometimes it feels easier to flee a situation rather than embrace God-given opportunities. This human tendency is natural because people don't like the discomfort that accompanies fear. And yet God doesn't provide opportunities for us to flee; He wants us to step into them.

Other people respond to fear by fighting it. They take matters into their own hands. Jacob did this in Genesis 32. God had called Jacob to go back to his father's land, but he was afraid that his brother, Esau, would destroy him. Their initial conflict when he stole Esau's birthright had never been reconciled. As Jacob prepared to return, he devised a plan to avoid Esau's potential attack by bribing Esau with a vast number of animals as gifts. Jacob took matters into his own hands out of fear, but he ultimately didn't need to do so, because God helped the two brothers reconcile. Sometimes when people fear God's directives, they'll take problems into their own hands rather than trust God's Word or promises. This, too, is a natural human tendency we want to be careful to avoid.

The proper response when we experience feelings of fear is to face the fear—to embrace it. We'll benefit if we get curious and consider why we feel afraid. This helps us begin to accept it for what it is and eventually overcome fear with faith. We should do the very thing Jonah and Jacob failed to do—trust God's leading.

When Jesus told Ananias to go visit Saul in order to pray for him and restore his sight, Ananias was afraid. Saul had been persecuting Christians, and from Ananias's perspective, it seemed like a death trap for him. And yet Jesus made clear to Ananias His intent to use Saul (who later became Paul) to reach the Gentiles. Despite the uncertainty, Ananias took the step of faith to follow Jesus's instruction. Sure enough, his willingness to embrace the moment solidified Paul's conversion to faith in Christ and forever changed the spiritual landscape of humanity because of Paul's newfound faith and relentless desire to proclaim the gospel.

In reality, trusting God helps us face fear and embrace His leading in our lives. When we trust God, we have no need to worry. We can confidently know that He'll take care of us, because that's His heart. That's His nature. He's our heavenly Father who wants us to trust Him. He wants us to lean on Him. He won't lead us to do something and then leave us out on our own with no help.

However, the enemy wants us to think we're on our own. He wants us to live with fear, because in doing so he has power over us. And yet our courage is a reminder to the enemy of his ultimate eternal destruction, and that he actually has no power over us.[40] Darkness retreats when we fearlessly step into what God desires each day.

Facing your fears may mean you push through the fear so you can embrace all He has for you. This pushing through your fear might come by way of counsel from others, helping you overcome that fear. For some, it means dealing with the past in order to conquer that fear so they're set free to fulfill the plans God has for them in the future. God wants you to walk in victory and freedom from the past, with confidence that you still have a ton to offer others.

What Ifs

Have you ever wondered what might happen if you step out in faith and you're wrong? Or what if it doesn't work? Or what if you look foolish?

Every situation is unique, but when you take a step of faith based on something you sense God has told you, He will honor your desire to obey and follow Him.

Here are some questions to ask yourself as you process steps of faith or consider a possible undertaking:

- *Is it in line with Scripture?*
- *Is it meant to build up the body of Christ?*
- *Is it free from your own self-serving motives?*
- *Does it seem right based on the counsel you've sought?*

If all these things are true, you can confidently move forward regardless of any "what if I'm wrong" thoughts.

When you're in tune with God and you're faithfully following His Word, you don't have to worry about what happens when you step out in faith. God won't leave you hanging out to dry. This was a fear of Joshua's, but God gave him this comforting encouragement: "As I was with Moses, so I will be with you; I will never leave you nor forsake you."[41] He promises to be with us every step of the way as we faithfully seek to fulfill His leading each day.

A variety of "what if" scenarios exist for all of us, but God gladly answers those "what if" insecurities with compassion and grace. He knows our weaknesses, and yet He still longs to use the willing heart, so we can strike our arrows with confidence and conviction.

So remember: You're most likely not called to live in a remote area of the world. However, God does want you to follow Him despite your fears. We'll never be 100 percent fearless, but we can lessen fear as our trust in God grows.

The next time an opportunity comes your way (which could be today), don't let fear stop you. Face the fear, grab hold of the opportunity, and watch God use you to make a difference.

CHAPTER 7

SQUEEZING IN

We live in a society that's busier than ever. Busyness has become a badge of honor for many. How often have you asked someone how they're doing and received the answer, "I've been so busy"? Instead of the traditional "I'm well" or "I'm doing great," somehow "I'm so busy" has taken over as the leading indicator of a person's status. It makes little sense as the best response to that particular question, but it clearly indicates the reality of life today.

We've never been busier than we are now.

In 1948, the U.S. government started keeping track of average hours worked by its citizens. Interestingly, the average person works about the same number of hours per week today as they did in 1948.[42] This means the workload for the average person is about the same, and yet the pace of life feels busier than ever.

So what has changed?

Technological advances and changes in the family dynamic are two of the biggest contributors.

Advances in technology have many benefits, but they've also increased the demands for our time and attention. People feel pulled in many directions with sounds, notifications, messages, and instant access to unlimited information. We've seen nothing like it before.

At the same time, the family dynamic has also changed the pace at which we live. The number of two-income households has continually increased over the last several decades. According to the U.S. Bureau of Labor Statistics, two-thirds of traditional families (married couples with children) are dual-income families.[43] Additionally, the number of single-parent homes has drastically increased.[44]

Whether single or married, when you add to an already busy schedule such things as children's activities, personal hobbies, recreation, and other extracurricular interests, people are running at an unbelievable pace.

Life just gets more and more hectic.

Nothing's Off the Table

A few years back, Ashley and I had a chance to strike our arrows together as a couple. Some friends of ours were facing a difficult time in their marriage, so much so that they considered divorce. This was an extreme shock to us. Everything had broken loose in their home, and they'd reached out for help.

I admit the timing of this was not the best. My work responsibilities had multiplied and were about to grow even more. There were several things to juggle on my plate, and Ashley was also extremely busy with her responsibilities. We spent our few free moments together as a family. The idea of Ashley and me helping this couple during that particular season wasn't even close to ideal.

The first conversation I had with the husband after they disclosed their situation served as a true test for me. He mentioned on the phone that he knew how busy I was, and he didn't want to impose on my time. In that moment, I had a choice. I could agree with him and simply limit my help to occasional phone calls, emails, and text messages. It was a perfect scenario. He was giving me a way out.

And to be honest, I was tempted to take it.

I couldn't do that, though. He was my friend. I wanted to help. We couldn't neglect the opportunity to invest in them during the most difficult moment of their marriage.

That initial conversation began a journey we would embark on together with our friends. This was an opportunity from God for Ashley and me to help them through a tough time. Although tempted, we didn't allow our busy lives to prevent us from fulfilling the purpose God had for us to strengthen our friends' marriage.

Were we busy? Yes.

Did it require hours of conversation? Yes.

That's why it's important to plan for margin. We couldn't allow our busyness to override God's leading and the opportunity to help save a marriage on the brink of destruction. In their case, God worked miraculously to restore their relationship, and they've continued to thrive as a couple. Looking back, we're so glad we captured that moment to help our friends at a pivotal time.

Let's face it, you can't just reschedule these moments for later. Few things have greater reward than knowing you can help people in *their* time of need. And that happens when you have the margin to embrace unplanned occasions to strike your arrows. God uses the willing heart, and He blesses the available life.

As we experience the option to step into an opportunity, a time limit generally accompanies that occasion. Inherent in the word "opportunity" is the root word "opportune," meaning well-timed or correctly aligned with the time and occasion. Each opportunity we encounter generally comes with a finite time to capitalize on that opportunity.

When people have their lives booked full, they might not see an opportunity from God, which is where creating margin comes into play. In reality, the tasks of life will eventually get accomplished, even if delayed because of outside circumstances. But divinely provided opportunities generally cannot be rescheduled.

> God uses the willing heart, and He blesses the available life.

Those who strike their arrows will wake up each day knowing God's agenda supersedes their own plans. Let's always remember that for God, nothing is off the table. We often plan for our future, but God might disrupt those plans with His plan, which is always best. Margin allows us to squeeze in opportunities from God that we weren't planning on.

None of us will hit the nail on the head every time. We'll look back occasionally and see how we missed opportunities due to our busy schedules. In these moments, we must give ourselves grace as we work to minimize our *busyness* in order to focus on His *business*.

The Schedule of Jesus

When the Savior of the world arrived, His new followers couldn't get enough of Him. God had become flesh, in person. This was the moment people had eagerly anticipated for centuries, and now the moment had arrived.

From early on, the schedule of Jesus was consumed with the Father's itinerary. When Jesus went missing from His parents at age twelve, we find the first recorded mention of His priority to spend time in the Father's house, attending to the Father's affairs.[45] After His ministry officially began, we see further explanation of Jesus's schedule. In John's Gospel we read these words from Jesus: "For I have come down from heaven not to do my will but to do the will of him who sent me."[46] Jesus's mission was to fulfill the Father's master plan, and He devoted every day to that agenda.

The demands for Jesus's time and attention were unlike anything any of us has ever seen. Everyone wanted a slice of His time, day and night. He was so popular that not everyone could easily get access to Him. One woman squeezed through a crowd just to touch Jesus's robe with her fingertips in hopes of being healed.[47] Another group of individuals had the brilliant idea to bust a hole in the roof of a home so they could lower a paralyzed man down right in front of Jesus.[48] People were desperate for access to Jesus.

The Gospels highlight only some of the innumerable activities during Jesus's ministry. John tells us, "Jesus also did many other things. If they were all written down, I suppose the whole world could not contain the books that would be written."[49]

Remember, Jesus's ministry lasted only three years—but He kept a full schedule throughout.

On one occasion, Jesus had just left Jericho and was en route to His next destination. Alongside the road was a blind beggar, Bartimaeus, who yelled out for Jesus. Immediately, many people traveling along tried to quiet the man. Given the popularity of Jesus, His being interrupted by a socially insignificant blind man was a low priority—so everybody thought. But as Bartimaeus called out even louder a second time, we see a powerful display of Christ's love, compassion, and priorities. The Bible tells us that "Jesus stopped and said, 'Call him.'"[50]

Immediately, Bartimaeus hopped up and went to Jesus. He declared his desire to recover his eyesight. In that moment, Jesus offered him the only hope he would ever receive, and he was healed of his blindness.

Despite His schedule, Jesus was always willing to stop and meet a need. The most sought-after man in human history had the margin to help the marginalized. He was never too busy for an opportunity to help someone in need.

Have you ever noticed how God doesn't operate on your schedule? Your inconveniences are sometimes God's greatest moments to shine. It's the moment when God drops a spiritual opportunity into your lap. You have the choice on what to do with that God-given opportunity.

The apostle Paul instructs us, "Therefore, as we have opportunity, let us do good to all people, especially to those who belong to the family of believers."[51] However, it's hard to embrace these opportunities when it doesn't align with our schedule and plans for the day. It's inconvenient to give up a Saturday for a day of serving others. It's hard to prepare and drop off a meal for a family in need when you can hardly meal-plan for your own family. It's inconvenient to meet with that person who just needs to chat when you've got a lot going on. It's inconvenient to do whatever God wants you to do when it interrupts your routine.

But as we know, God doesn't operate on our timeline, and He's not worried about our own agenda. He has His agenda as part of His divine master plan, and it's more important by far than anything we want to do.

Remember the Sabbath—and Slow Down

When Covid-19 arrived on the scene in 2020, nearly everyone around the world experienced life-altering realities. In 2020 alone, Covid-19 was attributed to having caused more than 1.8 million deaths worldwide.[52]

Government entities and organizations all over the world collaborated in an effort to slow the disease's spread and minimize the number of people contracting it. Cities, regions, and even entire countries shut down, forcing many businesses, restaurants, churches, and organizations to close. Many locations in the U.S. had complete stay-at-home orders for varying lengths of time. Countless numbers of people were laid off work, while others had to begin working in a virtual manner from home. It was a very tumultuous time for many. The disease created a new normal for much of society.

One outgrowth I observed during the intense Covid-19 season related to people's priorities. Many people noted how everything slowed down for them (and they actually liked the slower pace). With nearly all entertainment and extracurricular activities inoperable, people were forced to wind down.

Ashley and I used that season to reassess our personal values. We embraced the occasion to seek direction for our individual lives and God's desire for our family. It was a natural opportunity to evaluate our priorities. By taking the time to focus on what mattered most, God gave us clarity on personal decisions as we prepared for the next season of life and ministry that we sensed He wanted us to step into.

The regular and prayerful evaluation of how you use your time and resources will assuredly increase your stewardship and effectiveness. This was what Moses conveyed in prayer to the Lord: "Teach us to make the most of our time, so that we may grow in wisdom."[53] As we slow down and examine how we utilize our time, we'll no doubt grow wiser as we seek to make the most of it.

In reality, it's out of our rest that we give God our best.

God instituted the Sabbath at the beginning of time because people need to rest. God wants your best, which means that slowing down to refresh is a spiritually healthy necessity. Jesus alluded to this when He said, "The Sabbath was made to benefit people."[54]

If you've lost the joy of serving due to over-commitment, remember the Sabbath. Regular seasons of rest will edify and develop you. In doing so, you'll be more equipped for and aware of opportunities to strike your arrows.

Staying in Alignment

After serving as an associate pastor of two churches, I co-founded Leaders.Church to give pastors and churches practical online resources. One trend I observed throughout those various ministry experiences is that quite a few ministry leaders actually do too much ministry.

Can you believe that?

Did you know 90 percent of pastors work more than fifty-five hours per week, and 91 percent of pastors have experienced some sort of burnout in ministry?[55] Burnout often happens because pastors are doing too much.

If you happen to minister full time in some capacity, and your busyness is consumed with ministry tasks, you may be out of alignment with God's design for you. In Ephesians 4, Paul makes it clear that the leaders of the church are "to equip God's people to do his work and build up the church."[56] Leaders shouldn't fill their daily schedules with doing ministry. Rather, their job is to train, equip, and empower others to carry out the ministry.

If you find yourself in the weeds with too many ministry tasks, maybe you would benefit from doing *less*. As we read the Gospels, we see Jesus praying, mentoring His disciples, discussing important topics in-depth, bonding with others over shared meals, and continually reaching out to lost and hurting people. Yet we never see Him looking rushed, frantic, or pressed for time.

In reality, God doesn't intend that we hurry from opportunity to opportunity, wearily laboring for the kingdom. "Hurry" is the enemy of God. He wants us to slow down enough to simply be present in every single moment.

Jesus's life demonstrates that God provides all the time you need to do what He calls you to do without having to continually worry that you're not doing enough. It may simply mean it's time to begin leading at a higher level where you *equip* more and *do* less.

For those who attempt to minister obsessively at all hours, often to the neglect of spouses and families—imagine if you were to slow down long enough to ensure you heard God's call more clearly. What a difference that could make!

If we want to make our mark in this world, we must start with an honest self-evaluation of our commitment to God's kingdom purposes. To be sure, if we're lounging on the sidelines, we may miss the joy of stepping into God-given opportunities. But if we're in perpetual motion and we never take a break from "doing," now may be the time to reconsider our priorities.

God will accomplish His will and purposes on Earth with or without our participation, but we stand to miss innumerable blessings if we get out of alignment with God's design for our lives.

CHAPTER 8

EXTRAORDINARY FAITH

In 2013, our friends Scott and Jen Obremski felt led to start a new church in Kansas City, Missouri. Upon hearing about this new venture, Ashley and I sensed that God wanted us to go too. We knew God was up to something special, because He spoke to many people—individuals, couples, and families—about participating in the endeavor.

A total of forty-two people collectively struck their arrows through an enormous step of faith. Most of them lived in Springfield, Missouri, approximately three hours away from their soon-to-be new home city. Most left everything behind to start a new life.

Among them were our friends Jon and Heather Torgeson. The Torgesons were a young couple full of enthusiasm to see God work in big ways. Jon had grown up in Springfield while Heather was from western Kansas. After Heather moved to Springfield for college, she met Jon, and they were married within two years. When the announcement about the Kansas City church plant was made, the Torgesons were the first to join the launch team.

This was the biggest step of faith Jon and Heather had ever made. Jon immediately looked for any job he could find in Kansas City, not knowing anything about the city. After finding work as a custodian at the Kansas City Art Institute, he and Heather quit their jobs and prepared for the new adventure.

This endeavor was no cakewalk. The Torgesons left all of their family to go to a place where they had no family. This was especially hard since Heather was eight months pregnant with their first child. Some may have thought this young couple was making a foolish decision. Could they secure health insurance in time? How would they pay for the upcoming labor and delivery expenses during a job transition? Why would they leave their family support system for a church that was only a concept? It made little sense, but God was in it.

The Torgesons were the first to arrive in Kansas City, even before Scott and Jen. They knew the general area of the metro where the new church would be planted, but its exact location was not fully clear. Many unknowns still existed, but that didn't stop the Torgesons from stepping into the new life God had for them—even though they had no idea how that new life would look.

They secured a new apartment, selected a new ob-gyn, and began a new career all because God wanted them to help start a new church. Now that's extraordinary faith. They enthusiastically jumped in with both feet to embrace the unknown, and God helped them immensely every step of the way. Eventually, the remaining others made the move, and a thriving new church was birthed in Kansas City on September 15, 2013.

Belief

When we have faith, God is faithful. In fact, He moves in response to our faith. He honors those who live with faith. He'll take average people and do something exceptional through them, simply through their faith.

Sometimes people lack the faith to believe their actions will make a difference. They might cognitively know that God can use anyone or any situation to accomplish His purposes, but they don't actually believe it's possible.

Knowing and believing often get intertwined, but they're uniquely different. For example, the Pharisees knew who Jesus was, but they didn't believe He was the Son of God. They cognitively heard and listened to Him. They could touch and see Him. But they didn't actually believe that what He said was truth.

This reality plays out in our lives too. We can know something's possible and yet not believe it will happen.

Have you ever thought that way?

Maybe you know your family member could start following Jesus and you pray to that end, but you aren't sure it will actually happen. Maybe you know your conflict at work can be resolved, but you just don't see how. Maybe you know your consistent parenting will steer your child in the right direction, but you wonder if it's actually sinking in.

Knowing is different from believing. The key differentiator between knowing and believing is a matter of faith. Faith is hard to describe. It's intangible. It doesn't always make sense. And yet a little thing called faith is what moves people from knowing to believing.

And to take it a step further, faith is what makes the impossible become possible.

Jesus validated this truth when He said, "If you have faith as small as a mustard seed, you can say to this mountain, 'Move from here to there,' and it will move. Nothing will be impossible for you."[57]

> As you experience opportunities to strike your arrows, God wants you to believe your actions will lead to a great victory.

Faith makes anything possible.

As you experience opportunities to strike your arrows, God wants you to believe your actions will lead to a great victory. God wants you to expect that He'll work at any given moment to bring about the result He desires.

Overcoming Doubt

When we walk by faith, times may come when we doubt our decisions and actions. If you've ever had your faith dwindle, you're in good company. Even the apostles struggled with weakened faith at times, and they walked with Jesus every day.

When doubt sets in, it's easy to have our attention and focus placed on our challenges instead of our opportunities. As we approach a door that God wants us to step through, the situation might look bleak. We might find several reasons why it won't work or why we shouldn't pursue it. And yet God doesn't want us to miss an opportunity to strike our arrows because we lack faith. When God prompts us to take action, He always makes the way.

In reality, God wants to turn your life's challenges into opportunities. We simply need to trust His leading and remain faithful to His purposes. Pastor J. D. Greear puts it this way: "Faith is not the absence of doubt; it is continuing to follow Jesus in the midst of doubt."[58]

So how can we remain faith-filled when doubt creeps in?

Ask God to build your faith—before you do anything else. He empathizes with our weakness, and He understands exactly where we are. Verbalizing this reality alone can build our faith, but God also will answer if you simply ask. In Luke 17:5, the apostles said to Jesus, "Increase our faith!"[59] As you ask God to increase *your* faith, He'll help you overcome doubt and step into the opportunities He's placed before you.

Surrounding yourself with faith-filled people also builds your faith. Have you ever noticed how energized you feel after being around other faith-filled people? It's so invigorating! You can feel like you're ready to conquer the world, because the people with whom you surround yourself will affect the level of your faith. The Bible rightly describes this reality: "As iron sharpens iron, so one person sharpens another."[60]

At other times, when doubt creeps in, praising God rebuilds our faith. This helps us take our eyes off the perceived reality of our situation and to focus our attention back on God and what He wants for us. David in the Bible was masterful at rebuilding his faith. When facing extreme pressure, he often worshiped God to rejuvenate his faith and confidence, knowing that God would help him to accomplish His purposes even when the situation looked bleak.[61]

When God asks us to step into His purposes, our faith is often stretched. Just like the muscles in our body benefit from a good stretch, when God stretches our faith, it increases our effectiveness to His mission. Each stretch of our faith helps us go a little further into God's purposes, gaining a little more confidence, and believing a little deeper that He will help us. God wants to stretch your faith further so He can work in even greater ways through you.

When doubt shows up, don't give in to it. Persevere with faith even when all hope seems lost. God will help you overcome your doubt as you take your eyes off your doubts and focus your attention on the solution—God.

God always gives us the strength we need to fulfill what He wants us to do. There's nothing that builds your faith more than seeing God do something unique through you. He wants you to live out your faith and be filled with confidence in His ability to move in ways you never dreamed possible.

Beth's Healing

At age ten, Beth Wilder discovered she had scoliosis during a checkup with the school nurse. This routine visit was the beginning of a long road ahead for Beth.

The first few years adjusting to life with a curved back went so-so for her, but as she entered high school, the back pain became excruciating. Doctors had the solution—back surgery. They said that installing a rod in her back was the only way to fully relieve the pain.

That is, of course, unless God healed her.

Beth and her parents gave back surgery serious consideration, but the doctors said the particular surgery she needed would prevent her from all future athletics. Beth was a cheerleader and played on the tennis team, and she wasn't quite sure she wanted to give those up.

Through prayer and discussion, she and her parents agreed that back surgery wasn't the right decision for them at the time, but she continued to see specialists regularly to monitor her back. As the years went by, nothing changed. By the time Beth was twenty years old, the pain had subsided a little as she scaled back her physical activeness, but it never completely went away.

Beth resolved in her mind that she would live with a curved back her entire life. Yes, it was inconvenient, but she knew things could be far worse. Since her condition wasn't life-threatening, she embraced it for what it was, and she was at peace with that reality.

But God had a different plan for her, better than she could have imagined.

On one particular day, an evangelist was traveling through her town. She and some friends decided to attend the evening church service together. At the close of the service, the pastor asked for people to come forward if they would like to receive healing. Since Beth had resolved in her mind that she was destined to live with scoliosis, she remained at her seat.

Among the friends she was with that night, only one of them knew of her scoliosis. This friend leaned over to Beth and offered to go forward with Beth for prayer. While Beth initially hesitated, she decided it wouldn't hurt to get prayed for.

Upon coming forward, the pastor asked Beth, "Do you believe God can heal you?" Her hesitant response led to the pastor repeating the question numerous times. Each time he asked, her faith to believe grew. Surrounded by friends, along with the pastor and his wife, prayers were offered up to God. And in a fashion only God can do, Beth's back felt burning hot. Instantly, her legs and hips realigned themselves, her bones began to move, and God miraculously straightened her back—although she still didn't believe it.

The next morning as she dressed for the day, Beth fully realized she'd actually been healed. Normally when she put on her jacket, it hung crooked until she zipped it up. But this day was the first day of her new normal. The jacket hung correctly on her body—unzipped! In that moment, she realized for the first time that she had, in fact, been officially healed.

Her friends and family inspired her to believe, and God honored that faith. Despite resolving that she'd live with a curved spine, God finally answered the countless prayers for healing over the years, giving Beth a victory she didn't realize was possible. Her faith grew and she received a miracle.

Did you know that every prayer you pray is another strike of the arrows? Sometimes the answers to our prayers will come days, weeks, months, or even years later. And some prayers might not get answered until we arrive in heaven.

If you've prayed for God to move in your situation, but you haven't yet received an answer, keep praying. Even when it doesn't seem like God is working, don't let that discourage you. God's silence in a matter doesn't mean our faith is weak. And just because God hasn't yet answered your prayers doesn't mean the answer is no. Remember that God's purposes are greater than ours, and He often works behind the scenes in ways not yet apparent to us.

Our faith is expressed by our anticipation of the victory. When we believe God will work as we step out in faith, we can confidently expect Him to move in powerful ways. God simply wants us to believe in faith and to trust in His timing and in accordance with His will.

Mountain Mover

Arrow strikers are faith-filled. They live at the deep end of the pool. I admit that this life can feel scary. You might wonder whether you really want God to make a difference through you. Sometimes it feels easier to just play it safe. But that's not God's desire.

A writer at *Crosswalk* reminds us that when Jesus said mustard-seed faith could move mountains, He was "directing our attention not to the quantity or strength of our faith, but to the *object* of our faith. Our faith is only as strong as the object in which it's placed."[62] That's why tiny mustard-seed faith has such incredible power. The power is not in the faith itself but in the omnipotent God in whom the faith is placed. That's how mountain-moving power happens.

> *Our faith is expressed by our anticipation of the victory.*

You just never know when God might drop an impossibility in your lap that He wants to make possible in and through you. Yes, you might have to leave your comfort zone, but that's where your faith to believe will help. Your faith reminds you to lean on God, because He is actually the one who makes the difference. God simply wants us to do our part so He can accomplish His part.

God is looking for extraordinary, mountain-moving faith. He wants people with faith even as small as a mustard seed to believe He'll use them to accomplish amazing things for the kingdom.

No matter your present circumstances in life, I encourage you to be faith-filled. Don't let doubt settle in. Know that God can and will do something through your life every single day, as you have faith to believe in His power and strength to do so.

CHAPTER 9

TRIED AND TRUE

In the mid-1990s, I attended church with a man named Kurt Warner. Yes, that's right—the two-time National Football League MVP. But when we attended church together, he wasn't *the* Kurt Warner. He was just a regular guy who played arena football for the Iowa Barnstormers.

Nearly every Sunday, Kurt would sit in the second row on the aisle. I would sit in the third row. We shook hands almost every single week. Here I was, just a high school kid shaking hands with a future NFL superstar, the Most Valuable Player in the NFL, but I just didn't know it yet. Even he didn't know it yet.

Eventually, after unsuccessful attempts to make the NFL cut in the U.S., a door opened for him to play in NFL Europe. He wisely accepted this chance to leave arena football and play professionally in Europe. After just one season, where he dominated the league in passing yards, he finally got the chance he'd dreamed of—playing in the NFL for the St. Louis Rams.

Kurt served as a backup quarterback that first season on the Rams, playing in just one game of the team's 4-12 losing season. That next year, the start of the 1999 season, the Rams' starting quarterback had a season-ending injury. This positioned Kurt as the new starting quarterback, and he led the team to an incredible comeback season. In fact, Kurt dominated the NFL. He led the league that season in pass completion percentage, passer rating, and number of touchdowns thrown. This was quite the feat, considering it was his first season as the starting quarterback for the Rams. He then led the team to their first-ever Super Bowl win and was even named the Super Bowl MVP.[63]

Kurt was extremely gifted, yet he missed out on many seasons early in his career. He tried to make the NFL, but he simply hadn't been given the right opportunity. In all those earlier years—after a so-so collegiate career at the University of Northern Iowa—it almost felt like the NFL for Kurt simply wasn't meant to be. Since he hadn't landed any professional football opportunities, he took a job stocking shelves for a grocery store. The irony is that this MVP-caliber player hadn't "shelved" his talents.

Kurt's later start in the NFL was the culmination of his years preparing for the right moment. God had a unique platform He wanted to give Kurt. His faithfulness and persistence in those years leading up to his NFL career prepared him for that exact moment.

Kurt later said, "From the day that I entered the league, I always knew that football more than anything else was just going to be the catalyst to allow me to impact the lives of other people."[64] And that's what happened. Following that unbelievable storybook season, Kurt and Brenda Warner launched the First

Things First Foundation to help people in need. It was a chance for them to strike their arrows, made possible because he put in the time and stayed faithful with what was in front of him during all those earlier years.

If you're questioning where you are in life, maybe you're in a season of preparation. If so, it is not time wasted. Our preparation in life helps us remain faithful for future moments. As we face adversity, setbacks, or delays throughout life, God wants us to persevere and stay faithful. Our faithfulness with what's in front of us will later position us for what God has next.

A King's Faithfulness

Had King David taken the throne when he was first anointed king, he wouldn't have been ready for the pressures and challenges associated with kingship.

As a young boy, David spent his days on hillsides tending to the sheep. Day after day he faithfully looked after them, protecting them from predators. The Bible tells us he killed both a lion and bear, which is no small feat.[65] His exploits while guarding the flock gave him physical and mental toughness.

No doubt David spent many days talking to God. Solitude on the hillside afforded him numerous opportunities to sing and play music. Many psalms were likely birthed in the pasture as he looked after the sheep. All of that time was preparation for the future God had in mind for David.

David's first real test came while he was still a shepherd boy. On the day his father asked him to take food to his brothers— who were in battle against the Philistines—David probably didn't realize his upcoming assignment from God. But he was ready.

After getting the sense from the entire Israelite army that defeating Goliath was impossible, David appealed to his preparation when discussing the matter with King Saul. He clearly communicated that by the Lord's help, he would defeat Goliath.[66] David's tried-and-true physical and mental toughness from killing a lion and bear, along with his dependence on God from the time spent in His presence, uniquely prepared him for that exact moment. David knew the impossible could become possible.

Defeating Goliath was just the beginning for this warrior-in-the-making. Much of what he learned while leading sheep—and later while running from King Saul—helped him be the leader God designed him to be as Israel's king.

Divine Intersections

Seasons of preparation allow us to act when the right moment comes. That's why the apostle Peter said, "Always be prepared to give an answer to everyone who asks you to give the reason for the hope that you have."[67] Our preparation allows us to strike our arrows even in unexpected God-ordained moments.

Sometimes people get so familiar with their surroundings and the daily routine of life that they subconsciously stop looking for these moments of opportunity. Have you ever noticed that happening to you? Maybe it's the regular conversations in the break room at work. It might be the daily commute with your kids to school. It might be the weekly interaction with other parents while sitting on the sidelines at a game. It might be the weekly prayer time with others at church.

Everyone has their daily and weekly rhythms, and these are some of the biggest moments for God to shine. In fact, God most often does the extraordinary within our own "ordinary." He takes the normal situations of life and works through them in amazing ways.

The truth is that God wants to divinely intersect your life with another person's need.

We serve an omniscient God. He knows all and sees all. And He has uniquely positioned you right now—where you are, in this season of life—to be prepared and ready for that moment when God crosses your path with another person's need, in a divine intersection.

> *God most often does the extraordinary within our "ordinary."*

If you're feeling worry and angst at the thought of missing a divine intersection, let me remind you that we serve a gracious and compassionate God. He understands our humanity and imperfections.

If you've missed opportunities in the past to impact others, you're not alone. Everyone at one time or another has missed a divine intersection. Let's face it, we're human. And sometimes our humanity gets the best of us. But despite our inadequacies and missed opportunities, God wants us to pick our arrows back up and begin striking again. He's a loving God, and He still wants to use us even when we make mistakes and miss opportunities. These, too, are times of preparation, which make us even stronger and more prepared for the next time an opportunity arises.

Lullaby of Hope

In 2012, our friend Krystalle Wheeler faced an unimaginable situation. Like many women, she experienced a miscarriage. In her case, it was the second pregnancy loss in just eight months. This time, she had a stillborn child whom they named Gracia.

Krystalle endured extreme hardship through that loss. Her body went through uncontrollable changes (including physical pain from birthing the baby). She also faced death, grief, and emotional pain. She now had to plan a funeral instead of a baby shower. And yet, through it all she remained faithful to God.

Each day, she spent many hours pouring out her heart to God. She never felt angry at Him, but she did experience disappointment. She chose to earnestly seek God—praying, journaling, and meditating on the Word. In that season she needed God more than ever, and He helped her. Through her time in God's presence, He equipped her with strength to overcome the pain and step into what He had next for her.

On the day of Gracia's funeral, a group of friends gathered that evening in a home with Krystalle to worship and read Scripture. A friend had prepared a song called "Gracia's Lullaby," which she first played for Krystalle that evening. The time in God's presence was healing and refreshing, and it was also a catalyst for what God had next.

On that night, her friends generously gave her about $400 to assist her. Krystalle could have done whatever she wanted with that money. No doubt she deserved to pamper herself, after such extreme difficulties. But she sensed God had different plans.

Krystalle's openness about her loss revealed how many women

had struggled with the same thing she had faced. Her faithfulness to God during such difficult times positioned her to step into an unimaginable opportunity. God showed Krystalle how she could use her experience to encourage others facing the same situation.

She wasn't sure she could do it, but upon sharing the idea with her pastor, who immediately affirmed it, she felt empowered to take the step of faith. As a result, the Lullaby of Hope ministry was formed.[68] She used the $400 to buy materials and supplies for gift boxes to show the love of Christ and provide encouragement and hope to others who experience loss in the womb.

The first gift box was created and given to a woman just four weeks after Krystalle's stillbirth. And that was just the beginning. In that first year alone, seven to ten gift boxes were given each month, and it exponentially grew every year thereafter. So far, more than three thousand gift boxes have been distributed to women around the world—all because Krystalle remained faithful to God's purposes despite her personal life's circumstances.

God doesn't promise a comfortable life free from all hardship. Quite the opposite is the reality for many people, including believers. It's easy to shift that focus off God's purposes and onto ourselves when facing life's challenges. If you've ever faced depression, disappointment, dysfunction, pain, or suffering, you know all too well how hard that can be. However, God wants to use our life-events for the good of others. Our job is simply to remain faithful to His purposes.

Victory won't always come easily, yet faithfulness and persistence will enable those with hardships to connect with God's great love and power, which will make a lasting difference in and through their lives.

The Miracle Mile

On May 6, 1954, British runner Roger Bannister completed the first-ever mile run in under four minutes. No one had ever run a mile that fast—the four-minute barrier had finally been broken.

Ironically, one month later, Australian runner John Landy achieved the same feat, even breaking Bannister's record time by 1.4 seconds.

This led to a head-to-head competition in August 1954. It was a historic race. The two fastest mile runners in history—along with six other proven distance runners—would compete at the British Empire and Commonwealth Games hosted in Vancouver, B.C.

Before the first lap was completed, Landy had moved into a significant lead and held there steadily, with Bannister staying in second place, slowly moving closer. With a quarter mile to go, Bannister was almost on Landy's heels, both men well ahead of the other runners. The two leaders were pushing each other to their limits.

As they rounded the curve for the final straightaway, Bannister kicked forward and pulled around Landy's right. That's when Landy made the biggest mistake of his running career.

Like any competitor is tempted to do, he wondered where he was in relation to his opponent. He couldn't repress the curiosity any longer, and his desire to precisely locate his challenger led him to quickly swing his head for a look over his left shoulder. Since the track in that curve swung behind him to his left, that would give him the quickest view of whoever was behind him. But in the same moment that Landy looked, Bannister was speeding past his *right* shoulder, thrusting powerfully into the lead. Bannister stayed ahead to cross the finish line in first place.

A bronze statue of Bannister passing Landy still stands at the Empire Bowl in Vancouver today.[69]

Landy's desire to compare his positioning cost him the victory. He later acknowledged, "I would have won the race if I hadn't looked back." He was concerned about his opponent rather than just focusing on the finish line ahead.

In a long-distance race like the mile run, the contestants are free to pass each other on either side. The rules are different for a sprint. When sprinters race at a track meet, the rules require them to run in their assigned lane throughout the race to keep from disqualification. If they cross over the line, that's the end of the race for them. Likewise, God has uniquely gifted every person and given them a lane to run in—not so they can run someone else's race, but so they can complete the race given uniquely to them.

The truth is, God has uniquely designed you to run *your* race, not someone else's. He wants you to stay faithful to what He has exclusively positioned you to do.

Nowhere in Scripture do we find the same exact path for two or more individuals. The Bible says, "God has given us different gifts for doing certain things well."[70] Some people will have similar paths, but each path will have distinctive characteristics. He has uniquely created and gifted you to accomplish certain tasks now and in the future. What makes you most influential is your faithfulness to *your* path.

Comparison can distract us from what God wants us to do, because our attention gets placed on others instead. As we look at others around us, no doubt we'll find someone more gifted, more talented, more capable of achieving God's purposes. And yet if you sense from God that He has something for you, or if you experience a divine intersection, that means He wants *you* to step into it, not somebody else.

Be faithful with *your* path, and you'll see great spiritual victories. And you'll confidently know you've given your all to what He wants *you* to do.

Superstar Status

It's tempting to settle in as "average" when we're in seasons of preparation or when we compare ourselves to others. We might even be tempted to get a little complacent in our pursuit of God and of His will for our lives. But here's what you need to know. You aren't designed for an average status. That's not why God made you. That's not why He gifted you. That's not why God positioned you in your school, career, or environment.

The truth is, you were meant and created to be a superstar for God's kingdom.

God wants you to live like a spiritual MVP. He doesn't want your gifts, talents, resources, and opportunities sitting on the shelf. He wants you in the action, striking your arrows any time you can.

You are a Kurt Warner in the making. You might not realize it yet, but inside you have unique traits that God is planning to use, even if you think you have nothing to offer. God wants to help you discover and develop your special passion and gifts—and to look for greater ways to use them every single day.

If you're a nurturing mother, what can you do to better support your goals and calling at home?

If you're a leader in ministry, how can you better lead those in your local church to increase their faith and be more like Christ?

If you're a medical professional, how can you develop your skills to help those in need even more?

If you're a teacher, how can you increase your influence among the students?

And if you're a student, what are you doing now to prepare yourself for present and future opportunities?

No matter your career or present stage of life, your gifts have great significance. God can (and wants to) use you to further advance His mission.

> *Your faithfulness to fulfill God's design will lead to incredible spiritual victories.*

Your faithfulness to fulfill God's design will lead to incredible spiritual victories. Be faithful in your preparation seasons so you can step into what God wants at the right moment. Be faithful in meeting life's challenges. Be faithful to *your* path by focusing on what God has asked you to do, and God will honor your faithfulness to Him.

CHAPTER 10

WALKING IN SIGNIFICANCE

My wife is a remarkable woman. Early in our marriage we made the commitment to have her remain home as we raised our kids, and over the years she has sacrificially given so much of her time and energy investing in our three children, because God had spoken to her about her role as a stay-at-home mom.

Ashley could have successfully done a lot of other things with her time, but a high priority in the early years was playing with dolls, Legos, Monopoly Junior, and making slime. She knew this was the one chance we had to raise our kids, and she wanted to make it the best possible upbringing for them.

As a stay-at-home mom, she desired to make our home a safe haven. She put so much detailed thought into taking care of them, even in the little things. The kids felt safe at home. They felt comfortable. They never had to worry—all because of Ashley's commitment to make our house a home.

Several years into our parenting journey, something happened to Ashley. There was a unique moment when she heard from God, and that began a journey of processing her role differently. In the course of just a couple months, she had a complete shift in her mindset, all because God had a plan to use her in far greater ways than she realized.

From that moment on, Ashley's role as a stay-at-home mom got even more important. No longer was she to operate as the mother only to our kids; God wanted her to be a spiritual mother to many others also.

It took a while for her to develop into that new role, but she knew God wanted her to spiritually invest in our kids' friends and schoolmates and in the neighbors' kids. Some of them came from godly families, while others knew nothing about God. And yet God had uniquely positioned Ashley to invest in them.

The "spiritual mother" role was one of the many ways she struck her arrows. She took her present everyday moments to make small investments in our kids and the lives of other kids. All this happened because she shifted her mindset. She was no longer *just* a stay-at-home mom; she became a developer of many future world-changers. There's a big difference in those two roles.

Can you think of any mindset shifts that might help you more readily step into what God has for you?

On the surface, you may be just an employee at a store, or just a business owner, or just a medical professional, or just a pastor or a pastor's spouse. And yet down deep, God views your role as way more than that. He views you as His son or daughter created for special purposes.

A New You

Sometimes people limit their arrow striking because they believe they have little to offer. They may have insecurities. They might lack confidence. Or they may simply have a certain mindset about who they are, and they can't get out of that rut.

Did you know that 85 percent of the entire world's population struggles to accept themselves just as they are?[71]

Many people look to external factors to determine their identity, and this influences their perceived value to others. They find their identity in their work, relationships, achievements, or pursuits. And yet that's not God's desire for people, especially believers.

God wants us, as believers, to find our identity in Christ.

The Bible says, "Therefore, if anyone is in Christ, he is a new creation. The old has passed away; behold, the new has come."[72] When you put your faith in Christ, you have a brand-new you. Every part of your inner being is made new through Christ, including your mind.

You are now a child of God, and you have immense value in God's eyes. Paul affirmed this reality in his letter to the Romans, where he teaches that God actually functions as our heavenly Dad: "For those who are led by the Spirit of God are the children of God."[73] But that's not all. Paul also says we're "heirs of God and co-heirs with Christ."[74] This means that God hand-selected you to receive an inheritance. God loved you so much that He sent His Son to Earth so you could be an heir with Christ. You're extremely valuable in God's eyes!

Being an heir is a pretty sweet gig. First and foremost, you'll experience eternal life with God. But even now on Earth, every-thing God gives to Christ is something that we also have access to, through our faith. Yes, this means you have everything Christ has—including His power, authority, and confidence—to do whatever God might ask of you.

When you understand that your identity is in Christ alone, you can confidently strike your arrows as you step into God's leading each day. The realization of who we are in Christ will position us to do work for Christ. Your actions, words, and deeds are an overflow of your position in the family of God.

When an employee of a company acts on behalf of the boss, that employee's decisions and actions represent what the boss wants. Similarly, because of your position in the family of God, you get to act on God's behalf—with His authority—to represent Him among your family, friends, co-workers, and neighbors.

Now, we still may struggle or need help reframing our mind-set at times. The culmination of our past experiences shapes who we are today, including such things as our upbringing, life's challenges, and our encounters with tragedy or loss. While all of our previous experiences shape us for better or worse, let's always remember who we are in Christ. Faith in Christ makes having a new mindset possible.

The apostle Paul said, "Don't copy the behavior and customs of this world, but let God transform you into a new person by changing the way you think. Then you will learn to know God's will for you, which is good and pleasing and perfect."[75] This transformation of one's mind can happen instantaneously, but it's frequently a process for people as they grow in God through spending time with Him and other believers. As God transforms our minds, this helps us each day to determine God's will as we look to strike our arrows.

Turning Points

Several years ago, a friend of ours really struggled with insignificance. Every time she spoke with her family, she tended to spiral down into a sense of worthlessness. She became increasingly negative, and her negativity infused every situation she encountered.

This mindset resulted largely from her upbringing. Her parents hadn't helped her understand her value in this world. Quite the contrary, actually. They contributed to her sense of worthlessness—thinking she had nothing to bring to the table.

Then one day, God brought a spiritual mentor into her life. After several conversations, she slowly began changing her tune. Although she still had moments of negativity, she started realizing she had value to contribute. Her mindset began to change.

In a matter of just a couple months, this young woman who had felt so worthless and insignificant began to sense that God wanted to use her. And with that simple thought, she prayed about what she could do to contribute to the kingdom. After prayer and discussion, she decided to begin a Bible study with her mentor's help so she and her friends could grow closer to God together. She became an arrow striker.

That occasion was a turning point for her, and from that day forward, she headed in a different direction—a purposeful direction. She shifted her mindset. She realized her value. And God began to use her more and more.

Even if you've passed up opportunities or have inadvertently chosen to settle into mediocrity because you thought you had little to offer, God has more for you than that. He wants to use you. That's why you're here. You have something to contribute, whether or not you believe so. Maybe you simply need a turning point.

What's something simple you might be able to do?

It may be as easy as an act of kindness, an encouraging word, a special invitation, or starting a small Bible study group like our friend did. It can be that simple. Sometimes it's difficult to see our small acts of service making a difference, but let's always remember that no arrow striking is ever insignificant.

Truth be told, insignificance is a lie from the enemy. No one is ever insignificant in God's eyes. You matter to God and to the body of Christ, and you have more to offer than you might realize. It's time to walk in that significance. A slight shift in your mindset could be the single greatest key for you to grow closer to God, to maximize your opportunities, and to fulfill your God-given purpose every single day.

Eighteen Weeks Gone Bad—Except for One Lesson

On a hot summer day in August 2019, I took the kids to the pool. It was a chance to hang out with them, catch some rays, and loosen my muscles, because the next day I was slated to compete in an Olympic distance triathlon.

I'd completed several triathlons years earlier. However, it had been at least seven years since my last race. I therefore made sure to train properly for this triathlon, closely following an eighteen-week regimen. I certainly didn't want to "pull a hammy" in the race.

Unfortunately, all that time, hard work, and sweat went out the window the day before the race, when "the incident" occurred.

At the time, my youngest daughter, Fia, wasn't quite three years old. Our family was thoroughly enjoying the neighborhood pool—playing, laughing, and enjoying a fun time together. Fia and I were at one end of the pool while my older two kids were in the deep end, and Fia wanted to go down to them.

With her beautiful blond curly hair blowing in the warm summer breeze, she ran next to me with her typical pitter-patter while I walked alongside the pool. That's when the day changed for the worse. In a single moment, Fia cut in front of my path as I was swinging my left foot forward, only to hear a pop.

Being less than three feet tall, and weighing just twenty-five pounds, Fia was tiny but mighty. In a split second, I broke a toe when I accidentally kicked her little leg. Ouch! I curled up on the hot concrete in excruciating pain.

Don't worry. Fia was okay—but I was not.

It was the fourth toe, the one next to the pinky. I never realized how important the fourth toe is until I couldn't use it. After this mishap, I could hardly walk, let alone compete in a race. It seemed to affect everything I did. If you've ever injured a toe, then you know exactly what I mean.

Even the smallest and most insignificant parts of the human body have a function. And when they aren't functioning properly, everything else feels out of whack.

Did you know the body of Christ functions in the same way?

Every person who believes in Jesus is a part of the body of Christ, and each of them plays a part in the overall picture of God's purposes. Fulfilling God's purposes is the role not only of pastors and spiritual leaders. The Bible tells us, "Their responsibility is to equip God's people to do his work and build up the church."[76]

Spiritual leaders have their role to play, but it's clear that God has a purpose for every person in the body of Christ. The apostle Paul described this truth through an analogy of the physical body in his letter to the Corinthians: "But our bodies have many parts, and God has put each part just where he wants it."[77] In other words, God's people, including you and me, are responsible to fulfill God's purposes. He's positioned everyone where He wants them to be at this exact moment in time.

> *No matter what you believe about yourself, you do have gifts, and God wants you to use them.*

Sometimes people believe they're inadequate because they compare themselves to more "spiritual" people. They suppose that since they could never preach like the pastor, or because they don't know the Bible that well, they have little to contribute to God's kingdom. But the Bible tells us that God uniquely gifts everyone.

No matter what you believe about yourself, you *do* have gifts, and God wants you to use them.

God wants every believer engaged in His mission. He has a divine plan and purpose for everyone, every single day, regardless of what they think they have to offer. The apostle Paul alluded to this as he continued his analogy of the human body: "In fact, some parts of the body that seem weakest and least important are actually the most necessary."[78]

You have significance in the kingdom of God regardless of your family upbringing, spiritual maturity, or set of skills. You may not recognize your gifts, and you may think you have little to offer others. But as Paul points out, the gifts and skills you bring to the table might actually be the most important contribution to the body of Christ.

Maybe, just maybe—could the little that you have to offer be one of the most necessary things for someone close to you, such as a family member or friend?

Preparing for Action

Now that you realize you have a great deal to offer, it's time to prepare your mind for action—so that you can strike your arrows.

Your mindset can open up new opportunities, because you'll begin to see the possibilities of what God can do. The apostle Peter understood this when he told the early church to "prepare your minds for action."[79] Peter was a leader in the early church, and his leadership helped spread the gospel.

Peter's active command to first-century believers had the connotation of figuratively gathering up their long flowing garments so they could be ready for physical activity—just like a soldier would do when preparing for battle. In this case, it was a call to mental activity—being alert to God's will—in the spiritual battle.

Our mental fitness prepares us to strike our arrows. In order for us to make the biggest difference possible, God desires that we be mentally alert and prepared for opportunities. The more prepared we are, the more spiritual victories we'll see.

The spiritual exercise to prepare our minds for what God wants to do occurs in two settings: time with God and time with people.

Time with God

On the night of Jesus's arrest, He'd spent a considerable amount of time in prayer. That time alone with the Father was exactly what He needed as He prepared for the hardest week of His life.[80] Similarly, your daily encounter with God is the first step in preparing your mind for action.

Time alone with God has great importance, because it helps us get our mindset in the right place, and it prepares us for what's to come. Prayer reframes our minds. Prayer builds our faith. Prayer positions us to see new ways in which God may want us to strike our arrows.

If you don't consistently pray and meditate on God's Word, I want to encourage you to start doing so. This crucial routine will help you prepare your mind for action so that you're ready for what God wants to do next through you.

Time with People

Spending time with the people around us also prepares our minds for action. The Bible says, "Whoever walks with the wise becomes wise."[81] As we spend increasing amounts of time with wise people, we'll see an increase in our own wisdom.

God regularly uses other people to support and strengthen one another. Advice, encouragement, and counsel from others could be the differentiating factor in your ability to step into what God has for you.

Since all people are susceptible to mental obstacles, everyone needs guidance, encouragement, and help from time to time. In fact, one of my favorite verses from the book of Proverbs tells us how significant this is: "Plans fail for lack of counsel, but with many advisers they succeed."[82]

Counsel and advice often determine success or failure. God will regularly use the counsel of others to help us fulfill His plan. He frequently gives us the encouragement to step into opportunities as we seek advice from others.

This is how God designed the body of Christ. This was His intent in order to help us to collectively prepare for action.

As you get ready for what's next in God's will for you, know that your time with Him and your time with people will prepare you in ways far beyond what you could do on your own.

CHAPTER 11

BEYOND "YOU"

When Emery, our first child, was born, I had no idea the rude awakening I was about to receive. Every first-time parent probably experiences this reality. In my case, I had no idea it was coming.

Truth be told, married life before kids was amazing. We did just about whatever we wanted, whenever we wanted. Working out. Movies. Road trips. Sleeping in on the weekends. You name it, we did it—when *we* wanted. Then Emery came along, and I realized how life had changed forever.

Now, before you think I'm some noble person who was forever changed by the fact that I became a father, I have to be honest. Becoming a first-time father was a great experience, but the part that largely sticks out in my mind now is how inward-focused I was prior to having a child. I was actually a very selfish individual.

Everything was about us as a couple—and then, out of nowhere, *much less* was about just us.

Of course, like many newborns, Emery's sleep schedule was

rather inconsistent, and so was ours. We no longer had the choice of sleeping through the night, especially during those forty-five-minute episodes of endless crying at three A.M.

Talk about inconvenient, right? Emery clearly didn't realize we had work and other responsibilities the next day.

If you're a parent, you know this reality all too well. Having your first child is one of the best and most exciting aspects of adulthood for many people. It's also one of the most eye-opening and challenging parts of life, as we learn to take care of someone else's needs beyond our own.

Bucket Fillers

When my son Axel was in preschool, they taught him about two types of people: bucket dippers and bucket fillers. In other words, people either take from others or they give to others.

Bucket dippers focus on themselves. They look to see what they can get out of a relationship. On the other hand, bucket fillers look to see what they can *give* to a relationship. Whether sharing an encouraging thought, lending a helping hand, or meeting another's need, bucket fillers focus on others. While some people are naturally inclined this way, I believe God wants all people to be bucket fillers, including you and me.

God wants people to give their time, attention, and resources to helping one another. This sometimes conflicts with our humanity, which is naturally about us more times than we'd probably like to admit. We tend to look out primarily for ourselves, and we don't like it when things go contrary to our plans and desires.

This is a challenge for many people—but there is a solution.

Jesus acknowledged the self-focused behavior in humanity when He said, "Whoever tries to keep their life will lose it, and whoever loses their life will preserve it."[83] People can't live out the life Jesus has designed for them when *their* lifestyle, personal desires, and priorities take precedence over God's desire. That's why He told people to deny themselves if they truly want to follow Him.[84]

The apostle Paul suggests the remedy for self-interest is to help others:

> Do nothing out of selfish ambition or vain conceit, but in humility consider others better than yourselves. Each of you should look not only to your own interests, but also to the interests of others.[85]

Selfless living helps us overcome our selfishness. It's the antidote to our self-centered nature. Our awareness of others' interests in addition to our own helps us have greater love and compassion for people.

In his book *Absolute Surrender*, Andrew Murray pointed out this reality of our human nature: "One of the worst things sin did for man was to make him selfish, for selfishness cannot love."[86]

Since love is at the root of all good things people do for others, we must love others if we truly want to make a difference in people's lives. We can't fully help and serve others if we lack a love for them. Loving others compels us into selfless living, which then allows us to step into the everyday encounters God provides.

In reality, having an awareness of others is the key that unlocks the doors of opportunity in your life.

Yes, you heard that right.

Love and compassion for others is the way God uses people to make a difference. This type of generous lifestyle creates opportunities for us to strike our arrows, because our focus shifts from what we can get to what we can give—including our time, energy, and resources.

Living selflessly positions us to do good for others and to meet others' needs. That's why the apostle Paul said, "No one should seek their own good, but the good of others."[87] As we seek to do good for others, we'll experience great joy and fulfillment through our help, service, encouragement, and generosity.

Even science suggests the powerful benefits of caring about others. According to a report in *Time* magazine,

> Experiments show evidence that altruism is hardwired in the brain—and it's pleasurable. Helping others may just be the secret to living a life that is not only happier but also healthier, wealthier, more productive, and meaningful.[88]

However, the most significant benefit of living this way is the spiritual blessing you'll receive knowing that you honored God and attended to His purposes each day.

Unplanned Pandemics

In 2019, Alec Cook had just become the sole owner of Continental Siding in Kansas City. As a young entrepreneur, he was excited to take to the next level what the previous owner had started. That is, until Covid-19 hit.

As was the case for millions of people, this was a major blow to his morale—and his budget. He faced extreme stress and pressure knowing so many employees relied on his wise decision-making through this pandemic.

Fortunately for Alec, his business was considered "essential" and therefore remained open during the local shutdown. However, he had no guarantee business would operate as usual.

In fact, it didn't.

Alec saw an immediate decrease in business activity, and yet he felt prompted to do all he could to help the families of his employees. While so many families were in dire situations, he wanted to make sure everyone remained employed. Beyond that, though, he wanted to bless them financially.

After much prayer and reflection, Alec felt called to go above and beyond to help every single employee. He gave each person a 20 percent bonus during the pandemic. He also gave them a $500 "someone in need" one-time bonus check. Each employee had the prerogative to distribute that $500 to whoever they felt needed it.

Not only did Alec bless the employees with additional resources, but he even gave resources to help others who had no direct tie to his company. As a result, his company took an immediate hit in cashflow. However, he knew it would pay dividends among his employees in the months and years to come.

Alec could have hoarded the cash, tightened the reins, and not spent the money. Instead, he chose to give even more to his employees. It was a big sacrifice, but during such uncertain times, he felt that this was exactly what God wanted him to do. It was the perfect moment for him to strike his arrows.

Many spiritual victories came out of that single decision by Alec. He received countless stories from his employees of how they used the money to bless other people.

One employee, MaryAnn, took the $500 and distributed it to people from her local church who experienced financial hardship. She drove around town, visiting them in their homes. Each stop gave her a chance to pray with the individuals and give them some cash. Every single recipient was elated to see God's love displayed in a tangible way.

Alec easily could have focused on "me," but he chose to focus on "we." His decision to embrace that inconvenient and difficult season—to strike his arrows—resulted in many spiritual victories that would have a lasting impact on the hearts and minds of people.

The Biggest Inconvenience Ever

Jesus actually embraced the most inconvenient opportunity in human history. Having left heaven, He willfully came to Earth to live a sinless life and die on a cross. For who? For you and me!

None of His time on Earth was about Him, including His sleepless nights, constant verbal attacks, and ultimately, His sacrificial death on the cross. Talk about inconvenient! His entire life was a selfless act of love so that others might follow Him and receive eternal life.

I love how the apostle Paul described Christ's selfless act as he encouraged the church to follow his example:

> In your relationships with one another, have the
> same mindset as Christ Jesus: Who, being in very
> nature God, did not consider equality with God
> something to be used to his own advantage; rather,
> he made himself nothing by taking the very nature
> of a servant, being made in human likeness. And
> being found in appearance as a man, he humbled
> himself by becoming obedient to death—even death
> on a cross![89]

This is the model mindset for every believer. Just think about what God could do if people truly lived with this sacrificial mindset, where they willingly embraced life's inconveniences.

What if you looked at life's difficulties as an opportunity rather than an obstacle?

I wonder what this type of mindset would position you to do for God's kingdom. One can only speculate, but I suspect you'd step into new opportunities you never thought possible, simply because you embraced an inconvenience. In reality, the selfless act of embracing these types of moments is what God wants us to do on a daily basis.

Inconveniences will always exist. How we respond to them will determine our effectiveness.

At times, we all miss opportunities because of our instinctive desire to do our own thing and avoid inconvenience. In those moments, we can kindly remind ourselves that inconveniences will always exist. How we respond to them will determine our effectiveness. Embracing an inconvenient opportunity will likely result in temporary discomfort, and yes, your day may be a little out of sorts. But an arrow striker says, "Bring it on!"

Stepping into opportunities from God is by far the most important action we can take. Whether it's seeing a life transformed, meeting a need, or giving a little encouragement, these moments will yield God's blessing on your life now and in eternity.

When you reach the end of life on Earth, I hope you'll look back on life and recognize your awareness of others and willingness to embrace inconveniences—so you can accomplish His purposes in the lives of those around you. In the end, that's what matters most.

Breathless Expectation

As people look beyond themselves, the natural progression is expectancy. In other words, the next phase of selfless living is an expectation that God has an assignment for you right around the corner. Your job is simply to identify and embrace it.

Expectancy is being aware that God wants to use you, then being ready to step into His leading.

When Ashley and I attended Emery's preschool spring musical program many years ago, we met a brand-new couple, Tye and Jamie Murphy. The Murphys' daughter was in Emery's preschool class, and they'd become friends. However, we hadn't met Tye and Jamie until the night of the spring program.

Within minutes that night, Ashley easily connected with Jamie on "mom stuff." I quickly connected with Tye over our common work experiences. Both these conversations were delightful, and in both, the dialogue steered toward spiritual matters. Ashley and I each sensed God's nudge about inviting the

Murphys to our church, and we both extended that invitation.

Both the Murphys seemed enthusiastic and appreciative of the invite. Jamie had grown up Catholic but wasn't actively involved in any church. Tye had some past church experience, but it had been many years since he last attended.

It was rather clear to Ashley and me that they would come to our church. We knew it was going to happen—we expected it—we just didn't know when.

After months of praying for them along with additional invitations, the Murphys came to our church, and God began to work in their lives. In just a few weeks from their initial visit, they each made a renewed commitment to follow God. Then, at the next available opportunity, Tye, Jamie, and their son, Hayden, all got baptized to publicly express their faith in Jesus Christ.

I sincerely believe this spiritual victory was a direct result of our expectation in that particular moment at the recital—that God had a plan for this family. Truthfully, God is always at work in every situation.

I love how Oswald Chambers, an early-twentieth-century Scottish minister, describes this reality:

> To be certain of God means that we are uncertain in all our ways; we do not know what a day may bring forth. This is generally said with a sigh of sadness; it should rather be an expression of breathless expectation.[90]

We should eagerly expect and hope for some unexpected opportunities to pop up, because in these moments God shines the most.

It's a little ironic, isn't it?

Expect the unexpected! That's a given in the Christian life.

We know unexpected ways will come at any given moment—on any given day. Often dressed as inconveniences, these are opportunities for God to use us. When we live with expectancy, it positions us to more quickly step into what God has for each of us on a moment's notice.

CHAPTER 12

EYES ON THE PRIZE

The song "Eye of the Tiger" was released as a single in 1982 by Survivor, an American rock band. It was recorded that year as the theme song for the movie *Rocky III*. The simultaneous release of the single and the movie boosted the song's popularity worldwide. It held the top spot on the Billboard Hot 100 for six straight weeks and was the second most popular single of 1982.[91]

This inspirational song's imagery revealed in *Rocky III* defined the boxer's unwavering focus to take on his next opponent. It immediately became a pump-up song for athletes and sports teams everywhere. Athletes followed this newfound motivation as they'd listen to the song prior to competition. The song helped them to focus their mind and efforts on conquering their opponent, like a tiger who stalks its prey.

"Eye of the Tiger" can serve as a great mantra for anyone looking to achieve anything, because keeping focused on any task at hand presents difficulties. The human tendency for many is to drift off course, which is why our need for focus is so important.

When I'm driving somewhere with Ashley, I sometimes miss my turn or take a longer route than I need to. This actually happens more times than I'd like to admit. I always tell her it's our stimulating conversation that distracts me, but she knows better. Truthfully, I'm not focused on where I'm going, and I don't have the destination in mind when I start the drive. Instead, I get on autopilot, miss my turns, and aimlessly drive around the city.

Distractions can easily steer people off course in all areas of life, including our mission to fulfill God's purposes each day. Distractions might cause us to put our focus elsewhere instead of on the path God has intended for us. They might even hide a perfect opportunity or blind us from a divine intersection.

The apostle Paul understood this human tendency. He had an unwavering focus on the purposes of God and how God might want to use him on any given day. In his letter to the Corinthians, Paul used a boxing analogy to describe his need to keep his focus in proper alignment:

> I do not fight like a boxer beating the air. No, I strike
> a blow to my body and make it my slave so that after
> I have preached to others, I myself will not be dis-
> qualified for the prize.[92]

Paul is a perfect example of one who modeled steadfast focus. He understood that a person doesn't just jump into a boxing ring in order to shadowbox, which would feel rather pointless. Instead, a person hops into the boxing ring because they're going to fight. This same sense of purpose and intentionality was what Paul exhibited in his daily actions.

Paul wasn't suggesting in that passage that he literally beat himself up physically. Rather, that description revealed his need to focus on what mattered most. He wanted to keep his eyes on the eternal prize while keeping in check the temporary life he lived, including his earthly desires. He longed to keep things in their proper place, with eternal matters as the highest priority.

As we see throughout Scripture, that's how Paul actually lived. He faced all kinds of troubles in life. He was pressured, abandoned, and persecuted by people throughout his ministry. He faced multiple near-death experiences as he looked to spread the gospel, yet he kept a remarkable focus on the unseen eternal world. His mission to help others experience God was worth whatever temporary setbacks he endured.[93]

Any normal person would probably get thrown off by only a fraction of what Paul had to endure, and yet Paul never gave up. He didn't allow past experiences or present circumstances to stop him from accomplishing what God had asked him to do.

He articulated this strategy of unwavering focus in his letter to the church in Philippi:

> But one thing I do: Forgetting what is behind and straining toward what is ahead, I press on toward the goal to win the prize for which God has called me heavenward in Christ Jesus.[94]

Kind of sounds like an arrow striker, wouldn't you say?

Paul was a master at forgetting whatever distractions could throw him off course, while keeping his eyes on the prize. He had a goal to pursue, and nothing was going to stop him from accomplishing his God-given assignment.

Lifted

God wants us to remain focused on His purposes each day. That's why the author of Hebrews encouraged us to "throw off everything that hinders and the sin that so easily entangles. And let us run with perseverance the race marked out for us."[95] He knew distractions could be all-consuming and detrimental to our effectiveness for God, which is why he encouraged us to rid ourselves of those things so we could focus on God's plan for our lives.

Have you ever tried running with dumbbells in your hands? Or running while wearing a twenty-pound backpack? The extra weight you're carrying makes the run more like a jog, because it's hard to run fast and efficiently with that kind of burden.

That's the idea the author of Hebrews communicates in this verse. The word "hinders" carries the connotation of "weights." In other words, whatever's weighing you down, or whatever load you might be carrying, God wants you to throw it aside so you can live strong for Him.

As we purpose to follow God's leading each day, the cares of this world need not be on our plate. God wants your weights lifted. He wants your burdens placed on Him. He'll take care of our daily concerns as we focus our lives on following Him. That's why Jesus said the Father "will give you all you need from day to day if you live for him and make the Kingdom of God your primary concern."[96]

Now to be clear, this doesn't mean we can neglect our responsibilities and calling as a spouse, parent, employee, or friend. The challenge for some people is knowing how to prioritize these matters, along with all the other activities to which we devote time.

God has a greater purpose for us than achieving a certain economic status or portfolio size. He has more in mind for us than physical fitness achievements. He has higher priorities for us than our extracurricular activities. We can't live *only* for these things. These types of potential distractions shift our focus away from God and onto ourselves. God desires that we focus foremost on Him and His eternal purposes, and that we recognize that only He will supply every one of our needs.[97]

As we continually align ourselves with God's priorities, we'll find opportunities to step into what He desires each day. The art of arrow striking is knowing how to keep one's priorities in proper alignment.

> *The art of arrow striking is knowing how to keep one's priorities in proper alignment.*

This alignment of priorities is ultimately a matter of the heart. We speak, live, and act out of the overflow of what's in our hearts. So the ultimate litmus test for our priorities is our obedience from the heart. Are we willing to obey God when it doesn't make sense, or stretches our comfort zone, or requires great sacrifice?

Ashley and I had a real test in this regard several years ago. We sensed God asking us to give a significant amount of money to our church's fundraising campaign designed to expand the facilities so the church could reach more people. We fully believed in the vision of what God would do through these efforts, but we hesitated because God had asked us to give a lot of money.

The amount God asked us to give was the amount we had in our emergency savings. Giving this to the church would mean having no personal emergency fund—no backup cash for unexpected expenses, no margin for things to go wrong financially. It was a risky endeavor.

Naturally speaking, that made no sense to do. Who in their right mind would give all their money away? Well, apparently, we did. We confidently knew we heard from God on this one. It was clear as could be. God wanted us to drain our savings in order to invest in the ministry project that would reach more people in our community.

We could have easily justified giving half as much. It still would have been a significant contribution, and at the same time, it would have allowed us to have reserves for unexpected expenses. Nevertheless, we chose to honor God's concerns over our own. And you know what? Not once have we wished we still had that money. In fact, God replenished that money many times over since then. After giving away our savings, we had random checks come in the mail, unexpected salary raises, and huge provision through the miraculous acquisition of our home—where we made the seventh highest offer on the house at 32 percent *below* market value—and yet our offer was the one accepted. That's not supposed to happen.

Now I'm not suggesting that you run to the bank and withdraw all your money right now for your local ministry. But I know this to be true: When God asks us to do something, He'll provide the way for it as we stay in alignment with His desires and keep His priorities our priorities—not allowing the cares of life to take precedence.

No Condemnation

As a high school student, Jeremy Black began hanging out with the wrong crowd, and he quickly found himself heading down a slippery slope. Looking back, it was by far the darkest point in his life.

At age sixteen, he took his first sip of alcohol, but that was only the beginning—the gateway for other substance abuse that would follow. Within a few short weeks, Jeremy also decided to experiment with marijuana. In no time, these two substances became an addiction for him that took him deeper into a dark place of life.

Six months later, Jeremy decided to experiment with heavier drugs, including cocaine, ecstasy, and methamphetamines. Sometimes he would stay awake for two or three days straight with absolutely no sleep, as the stimulants flowed through his body. His body was wearing down, and his motivation for life declined.

Jeremy had some knowledge of God, and he knew his current actions were not God's best for him. He sensed that God had more for him than the life he was living, but the addiction was so controlling that he simply couldn't shake it. He was chained by the addiction, and nothing he could do would help him overcome it. All his efforts to overcome his addictions failed him, and he continued even deeper into that trap.

After three years of substance abuse, he decided it was time to end it all—that is, end his life. On an ordinary February day, Jeremy was coming down from a meth high when he made that decision. But before he proceeded any further, he had a sense that he should swing by the local youth pastor's house. Though he wasn't a close friend with this youth pastor, he felt comfortable enough with making a quick stop there. In that moment, he wasn't sure why he should visit him; he just felt that he was supposed to do it. Little did Jeremy know, that quick "drive by" would change his life.

Immediately, Jeremy shared the struggles and his need for God. He began sobbing, pouring out his heart to the youth pastor about how he wanted a different life. And sure enough, in that moment God delivered Jeremy, and he never touched those substances again.

Jeremy had intended to end his life that day, but God wanted him to start a new life instead.

That transformation began a journey God would take Jeremy on in living with purpose. As Jeremy was discipled and grew in his walk with God, he sensed that God wanted him to become a pastor. He enrolled in Bible college, then continued on to seminary. Shortly thereafter, God opened up a door for him to serve on the pastoral staff at a church where he got to disciple others who were new to faith, just like he once was.

Jeremy could have allowed the guilt and shame of his past mistakes to thwart God's plan for his future. Instead, he threw aside his past and moved forward into the future.

These same realities could apply to anyone who has ever made a mistake or committed a sinful act—that is, every human ever born, except Jesus. Thankfully, God chooses to use us despite our fallen humanity. If you haven't lived with purpose up to this point, or if you've possibly been living with some regrets, I have good news: God still wants to use you in the future.

It doesn't matter how big or small our mistakes have been.

The Bible says that because of our salvation in Christ, there is no condemnation for the past sins we've committed.[98] As was the case on the day Jeremy met with the youth pastor, "Where the Spirit of the Lord is, there is freedom."[99] The past doesn't have to taint your future. As the author of Hebrews pointed out, we *can* overcome sin in order to live out God's design for our lives.

The Judaizers

The leaders in the early church had some substantial mental hurdles to overcome. If you think about it, their entire way of understanding God's design for how they should live had changed. Prior to Jesus's coming, they followed the law of Moses. However, once Jesus had come, they no longer needed to follow the law in order to be in right-standing with God. Now they were free through salvation in Christ.

As you can imagine, that would have been extremely hard. Up to a certain point, everything they'd known and followed was directed one way. And then, upon encountering Jesus and His teachings, they had to pivot by living in an entirely new and different way. It was a major paradigm shift, and their way of living was turned upside down.

This explains why it was hard for the leaders in the church at Galatia to let go of some of the past requirements found in the law. Influenced by a group of people called Judaizers, they allowed their past way of life to distract them from the new way God now wanted them to live.

As a key leader in the early church, the apostle Paul challenged them to not allow these distractions to affect their spiritual life.[100]

Paul understood that a person's past life and way of living could distract them from the new life they had in Christ and their new purpose in life. It was hard to let go of the past.

The same is true for you and me today.

Have you ever felt that everything you thought you knew was actually wrong? Maybe you were raised to believe one thing, and then upon entering adulthood, you saw a completely different side to the story.

No person's past experiences were perfect. We all have pre-conceived ideas in how we view life and in how that aligns with our purposes today. Our upbringing affects our future, and so do our present circumstances. And yet God wants you to overcome these things—keeping your focus on His leading—in order to step into what He has next for you.

Welcome to the Future

God has more ways in which He'll continue to want to use you throughout your everyday life. As you keep your priorities in alignment with Him—keeping your eyes on the prize—and remain faithful to His purposes while moving forward, you'll find innumerable opportunities to strike your arrows. And you'll have confidence that your life is being used by God in the exact way He desires.

You can make a conscious decision today to focus on what matters most. Forgive and release the past, learn from those experiences, and embrace God's best for your life.

Always remember: God graciously forgives our past, and He joyfully rewards our future. Past sin, regrets, and distractions won't disqualify you from the future opportunities God wants to give you.

He has a plan for you, today, right now! Let this moment be your catalyst into what He has next for your life.

PART 3

GOING ALL IN

Every person has in their future what my friend calls a "rocking chair moment." If the Lord allows you to live a long full life on Earth, there'll most likely be a day when you retire from work. You'll have free time to relax, read, and reflect on life while sitting in your rocking chair.

Yes, on the front porch even.

The thought of sitting in a rocking chair on my front porch seems appealing even now. It feels simple. It feels relaxing. I can even picture my future grandkids and great-grandkids running around while I'm beaming, having a sense of accomplishment, reflecting on the legacy I'm passing on to them.

The way we live our lives matters as we prepare for that rocking chair moment. In other words, how we position our lives today will determine what we want life to look like at that time. This means you'll want your present decisions to reflect what you'll value later. Put another way, your actions *now* are preparing you for the life you'll have *then*.

For example, if you want a debt-free lifestyle with a substantial nest egg for retirement, then your preparation and actions today will position you for that lifestyle in the future. The only way to retire at your desired age, with your stockpile of preferred retirement funds, is to focus now on how to achieve that end result. This focus today will lead you to the rocking chair moment you desire in the future.

The same can be said of spiritual matters. Regardless of your current stage of life—whether you're a young student, already retired, or somewhere in between—God has a bright future for you. He has a bright future for you next year, next month, next week, and yes, even tomorrow. How we live today determines what God has next tomorrow.

In this next section, we'll look at the appropriate steps we can take to more effectively strike our arrows for God. You'll see how prayer, pruning, and pursuing can help you step into all God has for you.

As you follow that course—under God's direction and through His power—in the days, weeks, months, and years to come, you'll see Him miraculously work in ways far beyond what you could ever imagine.

Download a study guide for personal reflection or group discussion: www.arrowstriker.com/guide

CHAPTER 13

VICTORIOUS PRAYER

As a young married couple, Tyrell and Katy Reynolds were living their best life—the country life. They worked the family farm during the week and traveled to rodeos on the weekends. Tyrell was a successful team roper. He had opportunities to participate in rodeos all over the United States. At first, it was a lot of fun, especially with his successes. But then it became more mundane and routine. Every weekend, back on the road *again*. Fast-food eating. Subpar motel stays. Hours in the truck. Week after week.

As the years progressed, their priorities for life slowly began to evolve. Tyrell and Katy had an increased desire to settle down and start a family. Early on, they hadn't told people they were trying to get pregnant, but month after month passed with no pregnancy. Then, year after year passed.

They finally began to open up about their desire for a family, and those closest to them made it a matter of prayer.

Tyrell and Katy began seeing a specialist, and they started fertility treatments. Two years later, still no baby. Now, having made a significant financial investment to start a family, they were heartbroken and devastated. They couldn't understand why God had not given them the baby they desperately wanted.

At this point, they were more than five years into the journey of trying to start a family. For the first time, they began to wonder if having children simply wasn't meant for them.

That's when God showed up.

God had spoken to Tyrell's sister, Chasity Fritzmeier, about praying and fasting specifically for their situation. Chasity gladly followed God's prompting. She thought, *If God asked me to fast for them, surely He's going to give them a baby, right?*

Upon asking God how long she should fast, God clearly told her to fast for seven days. At that time, it would be the longest fast she had ever done. No food. Just water—for seven days. But it would be completely worth it if God answered their prayer.

This was a private matter between her and God. Only Chasity's husband knew she was fasting. She sincerely believed God was going to move, because He told her to fast. Powerful prayers were sent up to God. Day after day she called out to God, asking Him to give Tyrell and Katy the baby they desired.

Chasity had an urgency in her heart. Sometimes her prayers were quicker than she liked, but finding time to seek God amidst homelife had its challenges. And yet she prayed as much as she could, when she could.

On the seventh and final day of her fast, God spoke to Chasity with 100 percent clarity. It was so clear, almost as if He had spoken to her in an audible voice. "Chasity, call Katy and tell her she's pregnant—and that she needs to believe it." Elated by this word from God, Chasity immediately picked up the phone to call Katy.

Now, what Chasity didn't know is that Katy had been taking pregnancy tests on a specific schedule as directed by her specialist. Her last negative test was taken the day before this call to Katy (day six of Chasity's fast). So when Chasity told Katy she had been fasting, and she shared the message she received from God, she was initially surprised by Katy's melancholy response. And yet she didn't question what God had shared with her. Chasity stood on the message from God—that Katy was pregnant and needed to believe it. And Katy did, although with some reluctance.

So she took the pregnancy test again, just one day after having a negative test result. Upon taking the new test, Katy discovered she was pregnant!

Had Chasity stopped her fast early, who knows what would have transpired. She listened and responded to the voice of God, and God used Chasity to strike her arrows through fasting and prayer. Nine months later, Katy gave birth to baby Rhett.

Have you ever wondered whether a thought you had came from God or was just your own human thought? It's easy to ignore the subtle, small promptings we sense from God at times, because we question their source. Sometimes people excuse these types of thoughts, but when they do, they could miss out on what God might want to do in a given moment.

Our ability to make the most of every opportunity increases as we learn to hear God's voice throughout the daily routine of life. In Chasity's case, she could've easily questioned if she heard from God, but her consistent times of prayer and fasting over the years kept her in tune with the voice of God. Knowing when God speaks to us helps us strike our arrows by capturing divine moments and positioning us to serve one another.

> *Time spent in the presence of God is the simple key to unlocking His voice in your life.*

Developing a sensitivity to God's voice isn't as hard as you might think. Time spent in the presence of God is the simple key to unlocking His voice in your life. The more you commune with God, the more you'll know Him. The more you know Him, the more closely your actions will align with His desires.

What Did Jesus Do?

When you think of Jesus's life, many notable highlights probably come to mind. Here's a sample top-ten list of His actions:

- *Making the lame walk*
- *Giving sight to the blind*
- *Casting out demons*
- *Raising people from the dead*
- *Walking on water*
- *Performing miracles*
- *Teaching huge crowds of people*
- *Dying on the cross*
- *Rising from death*
- *Ascending to heaven*

These extraordinary moments that the Gospel writers high-lighted help people remember the life of Jesus. But hidden in the Gospels is another action of Jesus. One could argue that this action had the greatest significance—possibly Jesus's highest priority throughout His ministry. Yet it rarely makes people's top-ten list of Jesus's greatest moments.

What is it, you wonder?

It was His time spent with His Father.

Did you know the Son of God regularly spent time in the presence of the Father? Scripture gives us small glimpses of these moments, and we can learn a lot about the importance of time spent with God by looking at the life of Jesus.

We know that "Jesus often withdrew" to quiet places for prayer.[101] This was a regular occurrence for Him, and He often did so for extended periods of time—even all night long.[102] Prayer was a priority for Jesus. Regardless of the busyness of ministry and demands for His time and attention, He carved out time to commune with the Father.[103]

Prayer helped Jesus faithfully follow and fulfill the Father's plan. He earnestly sought the Father because He desperately needed the Father. As a result, His time in the Father's presence maximized His ministry on Earth. Prayer was the source of His strength to finish what He came to do.

The disciples also had a similar type of relationship as they communed with Jesus. Upon calling them to follow Him, their new priority was to *be* with Jesus.[104] They were His regular companions, and He prepared them for the tasks He wanted them to accomplish. Subsequently, many people recognized the disciples' actions and impact simply because they'd been with Jesus:

The members of the council were amazed when they saw the boldness of Peter and John, for they could see that they were ordinary men with no special training in the Scriptures. They also recognized them as men who had been with Jesus.[105]

In the same way, our daily lives will have greater impact when we spend time with God. Like the disciples, sometimes we simply need to *be* with Him so we can fulfill what He wants us to do. If the Son of God had to spend time in the presence of the Father, how much more do we need extended time in God's presence. You'll see the fruit of being in His presence as you live out your daily life with purpose and intentionality.

It All Starts with Prayer

When three-month-old Jalina stopped breathing, prayer was the only hope Justin and Jen Poindexter had left. Justin performed chest compressions, while Jen called 911. It was the longest minute of their life, and it led to several weeks in the hospital. While shocking in some respects, this wasn't much of a surprise, because Jalina had been dealt a pretty difficult hand at birth.

On her first day of life, the test results in the neonatal intensive care unit revealed that Jalina had multiple harmful substances in her body. Born with methamphetamines, cocaine, marijuana, alcohol, and Adderall, she was destined for failure. And yet, God knew that well in advance.

You see, in the years leading up to this very moment, God had planted seeds in the Poindexters' hearts about becoming foster parents. They'd kept it in mind for several years, but there was one special occasion that Justin has declared to be the defining moment for when they knew God wanted them to take the step to foster a child. God clearly spoke to Justin in prayer as he reflected on what he'd been reading in the Bible. It was now time for the Poindexters to strike their arrows.

God wanted this for them, and He had the perfect little girl who needed their tender love and warm embrace. Their home was the perfect place to recover from the substance abuse she endured while developing in the womb. More than that, however, the Poindexters would become her permanent home as God led them to adopt her into their family.

This little girl's life was forever changed simply because Justin and Jen listened and responded to the voice of God. However, that didn't mean it was always easy early on. When faced with sleepless nights and hospital stays, it was prayer that helped them hold on to what they knew God wanted for Jalina. God had a special plan for her. He had a purpose for this little one beyond just surviving life. He wanted to give her a bright future, and the permanent adoption into the Poindexter home was exactly what God had intended for her all along.

Before people rush into any kind of unique ministry opportunity, whether personal or professional, it's essential to know what God has asked and gifted them to do. Of course, everyone should be devoted to acts of kindness: delivering meals, making calls, sending cards, doing home or car repairs, and so forth. But through prayer, God may direct us to get more involved, to shift priorities, or to pursue a specific calling. Through prayer, He reveals His presence, power, and purpose.

In reality, prayer connects us to the heart of God and what He desires for our lives. Prayer leads us to take certain steps that He reveals in His timing. There's usually not a conveniently "good" time to step into what God asks you to do. Often the request by God to step into a new chapter will come during seemingly inopportune times. Frequently, people would like more favorable circumstances before they're ready to do what God asks of them.

> Prayer connects us to the heart of God and what He desires for our lives.

And yet when it comes to matters that are close to the heart of God, every moment is the right time.

The more in tune we are to God, the more connected we are to His heart. The converse is also true. The less in tune we are to God, the more we aimlessly walk through life. Scripture makes it clear: "If people can't see what God is doing, they stumble all over themselves; but when they attend to what he reveals, they are most blessed."[106]

When you aren't connected to the heart of God and you don't see what God is up to, this proverb describes how you'll stumble through life. Your time and energy can easily be misused, and you'll go through daily life wandering aimlessly, without focusing on His greater purpose. However, it doesn't have to be that way.

This wise proverb also gives us good news. God provides a way to maximize the spiritual blessing in our lives. We simply need to attend to what He reveals to us, and that will only happen when we regularly spend time with Him. The candid conversations we have with God help align our priorities, which easily can get off track. Through these moments of communion with God, our priorities reunite, and His desires become our own.

Sometimes people struggle to know the nature of their thoughts. They sense that God might want to use them in some way, but they question whether it's their desire or God's desire. That's why frequent conversations with God are so important. The more time spent in His presence increases your confidence that what you've sensed is, in fact, from God.

As your desires and priorities align with God's desires and priorities, you can confidently move forward with courage and boldness to seize that which you think might be from God, because you know you're in tune with Him. He has revealed Himself and His priorities to you, and your job is simply to attend to those matters to the best of your ability, even if that means stepping out of your comfort zone.

Prayer gives us the strength we need when facing difficulties. Prayer keeps us faithful when we lose focus, grow weary, and question our actions.

When Justin and Jen were in the hospital for weeks with a baby coming off drugs, no doubt they faced moments when they questioned God's will. Did they hear correctly from God about this little girl?

The Bible encourages us to "follow the Holy Spirit's leading in every part of our lives."[107] When you draw close to God through prayer, you'll remain assured of your decisions and actions to follow His lead, even when it doesn't make sense or your faith feels weak. As you learn to stay in step with God's Spirit, your efforts to minister in special ways will become more effective and satisfying, allowing you to live a most blessed life.

CHAPTER 14

PRUNING SEASON

Did you know the lifespan for the average American is 78.8 years?[108] For women in the U.S. the average is about 81 years, while for men it's 76 years.[109]

We're all given 24 hours every day; multiply that by 365 days, and it means we all have 8,760 hours to live each year. This means that on average, every American can expect to live somewhere around 700,000 hours between their very first breath and their very last.

That's a lot of hours.

According to someone's calculation published by the *Huffington Post,* the average 80-year-old will have spent the majority of his or her time as follows:[110]

- *26 years sleeping*
- *7 years trying to sleep*
- *13 years at work*
- *8 years watching TV*

- *5 years eating*
- *3 years on social media*
- *3 years on vacation*
- *1 year exercising*
- *1 year socializing*

Crazy, isn't it?

And that doesn't even include all the years doing miscellaneous activities.

Some of these figures might surprise you. Others may not. They say a lot about the average person's habits and priorities.

In reality, it's easy to get stuck in the routines of life. Let's face it, we're creatures of habit. We often do the same predictable activities without blinking—day after day, week after week, month after month.

Have you given consideration lately to how you spend *your* hours?

God wants you to maximize your time and steward your resources. We can best achieve this through evaluation. Since He seeks to increase your opportunities—because He has more He'd like to do through you—our assessment of how we use our time, energy, and resources can help ensure that we remain effective in fulfilling all of God's purposes for us.

The Power of Pruning

Scott Shelton has lived a pretty typical Christian life. He's a strong family man, heavily involved in the church, and an overall great guy. He's also an arrow striker.

Several years ago, he and his wife were midway through a Daniel fast when they decided to change things up. They felt as though they were simply going through the motions with more of a diet than an actual fast. Upon reflection of what to do, they felt they should completely eliminate TV for the remainder of their fasting period. Similar to the typical American, they would click on the TV for a couple hours after getting the kids to bed each night. While TV wasn't a necessity for them, eliminating it forced them to utilize their hours differently.

Shortly after cutting out the TV, they began to see a difference in their family. Scott and his wife started doing a devotional together at night. This helped them grow even closer to the Lord and to each other.

As a result of Scott's extended time in the presence of God, his sensitivity to the Lord's leading grew. In a matter of days, Scott sensed the need to help out with the local Big Brothers, Big Sisters organization.

At that time, Big Brothers, Big Sisters had kids on the waiting list to receive an adult mentor. Scott felt prompted to look into this further, only to find out that they needed adults to give only two hours twice a month. Yes, *only four hours per month.*

Scott immediately realized his time spent watching TV in the months to come could easily be replaced with the time spent investing in a young boy's life. In one year, he would use only 48 of his 8,760 hours at Big Brothers, Big Sisters. However, those 48 hours would be some of his best and most productive, as he made a difference in a young boy.

Pruning helps us strike our arrows more frequently. In Scott's case, pruning gave him the opportunity to invest in a boy who didn't have a father. He became a father figure to that young boy and showed him God's love in a practical way. Through that experience, the boy learned what a godly man looks like, and Scott was a visual representation of our loving heavenly Father. All this came about because Scott had the willingness to prune his life.

Every plant lover understands the power of pruning. When gardeners prune dead branches or wilted leaves, they cut them out to make room for healthy new growth. Spiritual pruning works in much the same way. When you cut unnecessary things from your life, you have room for something better that God has for you.

Pruning allows people to more effectively step into whatever God wants to do through them. Jesus acknowledged this:

> I am the true vine, and my Father is the gardener.
> He cuts off every branch in me that bears no fruit,
> while every branch that does bear fruit he prunes so
> that it will be even more fruitful.[111]

This is such great news! God wants you to thrive and be even more fruitful. He'll bear incredible fruit through you as you live out your faith.

As He did with my friend Scott, God will make it clear how He desires to prune areas of your life so you can step into what He has next for you.

Can you think of any areas of life that might benefit from a little pruning right now?

Just imagine what shifting one hour per week from unnecessary tasks to spiritually productive opportunities would do for the kingdom of God. That's 52 new hours per year that you'd now devote to kingdom purposes.

Can you take 52 of your 8,760 hours each year to serve your local church, a youth organization, or a women's shelter? That's barely more than half of 1 percent of your total yearly hours (0.6 percent to be exact).

And to be clear, we're talking only about *your* time. Multiply that by millions of Christians all over the world, and we're bound to see some major changes in families, workplaces, schools, and communities as people seek opportunities to strike their arrows.

Absolute Surrender

Pruning necessitates action. It doesn't just happen on its own. Intentional decisions to prune your life, habits, and priorities will help you stay passionately committed to the purposes of God. At any given moment, God may prompt you to change your habits or challenge you to grow. He does this so you can be more effective with the opportunities He wants to give you.

God is the ultimate pruner. And yet, since our relationship with God functions like a partnership, we also play a part in the pruning process. It's not just His job to change and mold and shape us. We also can take practical steps to reprioritize our time, energy, and resources to remain in alignment with God's design.

The key to effective pruning simply involves a mindset of surrender. God wants the entirety of your life devoted to His purposes. That's what helps you maximize your value to God's master plan. This includes your time, resources, energy, focus, habits, and priorities. It encapsulates everything. God delights in our willingness to surrender everything to Him.

In *Absolute Surrender*, Andrew Murray said, "The condition for obtaining God's full blessing is *absolute surrender* to him."[112] Complete submission to God is the gateway to His blessing in your life. You have infinite possibilities of how God can work in and through you when you live fully devoted to Him.

> **Complete submission to God is the gateway to His blessing in your life.**

This mindset reminds me of one of America's best distance runners, Steve Prefontaine. "Pre" was dominate in the early 1970s, setting multiple American records in long-distance races.[113] He pushed hard every single day, giving all his energy and strength in order to be the best. And he was. One of his most notable quotes still admired by athletes today is this: "To give anything less than your best is to sacrifice the gift."[114] While very true for any athlete, it also has profound implications for the Christian life.

Surrendering everything to God may stretch you, or get you out of your comfort zone, or cause you to give up something you enjoy. But there's nothing more rewarding than giving everything to God as you pursue the spiritual victory. That's what arrow striking is all about.

You've been gifted by God to accomplish His purposes, and He wants your best. He wants you to daily commit your time, energy, and resources to His eternal design. Giving your entire being to God is by far the most rewarding and impactful journey you could ever imagine, and God will honor you for your commitment to Him.

I Want to Be Like Jesus

Have you ever seen the 1992 Gatorade TV commercial featuring former NBA superstar Michael Jordan? The commercial implied that if you want to be like Michael Jordan, you should drink Gatorade like Michael Jordan does. I can still hear the branded jingle now. "I want to be like Mike!"

Honestly, it would be amazing to be like Michael Jordan in a lot of ways. He was hands down the world's best basketball player in history. He had many amazing achievements. He's also the richest NBA player of all time with a net worth of over $1.6 billion.[115] Jordan even has a world-renowned apparel brand. Humanly speaking, he's a successful man whom many aspire to follow.

However, as Christians, there's someone we want to be like even more than a successful man like Michael Jordan, and that's Jesus. Jesus was perfect. He was smart, patient, and compassionate yet strong. He was resolute and determined in His purpose on Earth, and He flawlessly accomplished the mission given by the Father.

The character and attributes of Jesus are amazing and something every Christian should strive to follow. But do we *really* want to be like Jesus? I think most people like the idea of being like Jesus, but when you think about it, being like Jesus is not glamorous.

Jesus grew up in the undesirable small town of Nazareth, which had a poor reputation. He had friends who were unimpressive and uneducated. He had a lot of people who disliked Him. And His death was rather unpleasant.

Why would anyone want to be like Jesus?

Well, it's because in God's paradigm, our hearts and actions mean everything, whereas our human achievements and resources mean nothing. That's why the apostle Paul told us to model our lives after Jesus, who "made himself nothing, taking the very nature of a servant."[116]

A servant's mindset is the desirable attribute for every Christian. In fact, this is another key component of the pruning process. If believers want to continually strike their arrows with effectiveness, following the example of Jesus and possessing a servant's mindset will help them do so. Now, this isn't easy. It requires a posture of humility, where you're willing to prune even good things in order to experience the best.

We know Jesus came to serve others and not to be served Himself. His purpose on Earth was 100 percent about saving lives, and nothing more. The apostle Paul also modeled this way of living when he said,

> My life is worth nothing to me unless I use it for
> finishing the work assigned me by the Lord Jesus—
> the work of telling others the Good News about the
> wonderful grace of God.[117]

As you emulate these examples of servanthood, you'll discover more doors of opportunity that God wants you to walk through.

Heart and Soul Nutrition

If you've ever talked with someone about pruning a plant, one of the things you're almost guaranteed to hear is the recommendation to apply a fertilizer to bolster its nutrients and encourage new growth. After pruning, you have to care for it tenderly and nourish it well for it to mature. Having proper nutrition will help it flourish into a beautiful plant.

The pruning process in our lives acts in a similar manner. Just like with a plant, proper nourishment keeps us spiritually healthy. As we feed our heart and soul, God helps us be more like Christ.

So what does heart and soul nutrition look like?

The gateway to heart and soul nutrition is your mind. What people put in their minds will affect their lives. This nutrition involves filling your mind with things that will help you and not hurt you. That's why the apostle Paul was so adamant about helping people's mindsets in his letters to the early church:

> Fix your thoughts on what is true, and honorable, and right, and pure, and lovely, and admirable. Think about things that are excellent and worthy of praise.[118]

The Bible instructs us to dwell on things that will draw us closer to Him and feed our spirit—to fill our mind with things that honor Him. If you've experienced negativity, doubt, disappointment, or failure, these types of thoughts can discourage you, weaken your faith, and minimize your impact. But God has more for you. He wants you to be encouraged with hope, expectation, and purpose—which is why the Bible also says, "Let heaven fill your thoughts. Do not think only about things down here on Earth."[119]

A healthy mindset is essential in the pruning process. Your ability to help, serve, and give to others will exponentially flourish as you nourish your spiritual life. As Paul also taught us, when we renew our mind each day, we can accomplish God's will.[120]

Set your mind and position your focus on God and His Word. This mindset will keep the focus off you and on our Master, and you'll be prepared to step into what He has next for you on any given day.

CHAPTER 15

A PROACTIVE PURSUIT

Austin Holt is a Christian entrepreneur. Over the years he has transacted real estate deals, owned multiple businesses, and consulted countless individuals and organizations in a variety of professions, including churches and ministries. In a more recent endeavor, he and his wife, Rachel, have started helping people with their marriages.

The Holts have a passion for helping people heal childhood wounds that manifest in the marriage relationship. They've counseled people one on one, hosted marriage retreats at their home, and built an online community to bolster marriages everywhere.

On one particular day, Austin had an innovative idea he felt God had dropped in his lap. It was as if God had given him a divine download of information. As soon as it came, he hurried home to capture the idea, which instantaneously flowed from his mind to paper. In a single day, a new, innovative way to help marriages was born.

His idea? A card game for married couples to grow closer in

emotional connection.

These Connection Cards would give couples the chance to engage in the types of conversations couples normally wouldn't even think to have.[121] The cards have a partially created sentence that one person completes, and then their spouse would respond with certain prompts.

Ashley and I have used these cards, and they're actually quite fun as well as enlightening.

Most people don't know how tenaciously Austin pursued this idea. When he sensed the idea from God to create these cards, he didn't wait for the right timing. He didn't put it on his eventual to-do list. Rather, he cranked it out immediately. Only three weeks transpired from the inception of the idea to the first batch of printed card decks. He had the idea and pursued it. He started strong and finished strong.

Austin's pursuit of the Connection Cards was a moment for him to strike his arrows. This unique and God-given idea was a simple way to strengthen people's marriages, and it worked. In less than a year, churches, pastors, counselors, and therapists all over the United States began using the cards as part of their marriage enrichment.

His immediate action on that opportunity has given countless marriages a second chance. Many who were headed toward divorce attributed the cards to helping them experience a complete 180-degree turn in their relationships. Couples everywhere experienced victory in their marriages because of Austin's proactive pursuit.

When people proactively pursue opportunities, they open the door for greater impact. Whether you have a divine download like Austin, or an idea just comes to your mind, God wants you to get going—to strike your arrows.

The best way to create opportunities is to embrace each moment. This might include initiating opportunities, or acting on ideas that come, or simply looking and listening for the next chance to make a difference.

Spiritual Goals

Over the years, I've set a lot of different goals for my life—for athletic performance, recreational activities and hobbies, finances, and personal growth. Some of these I've already achieved, while others are still in the queue. With my competitive drive and overall disposition, I enjoy achieving goals.

On a warm, sunny day many years ago, I had an aha moment while out on an easy run. I was thinking about my goals to race in the Boston Marathon and to complete an Ironman triathlon. While thinking on these goals, the Lord prompted a clear thought that changed my perspective on spiritual matters.

I thought, *What are my spiritual goals?*

At the time, I had spiritual goals—sort of. I followed a Bible reading plan, I spent time in prayer on a daily basis, and I fasted regularly. While these are good, I have to admit that the Lord opened up a new realm of spiritual goal setting I hadn't previously considered.

How many people would I strive to share with about Jesus in the coming year? Or to make it even easier on myself, how many people would I invite to church in the coming year? Or how many times would I serve at my church? When would I help the local food pantry? How much would I give to my missionary friend?

This wasn't hard, and yet I'd never before made official goals like these. Why not? Why wouldn't I want to seek more opportunities to do something great for God, even if it's a small thing?

What I realized in that moment was that I'd been aiming at nothing. For several years prior to that moment, I hadn't invited people to church, nor had I been sharing my faith with unbelievers. You've probably heard the old saying that if you aim at nothing, you'll hit it every time. Well, that was me.

In reality, spiritual goals can help us step into future opportunities from God, because the goal centers our focus on spiritual matters. Spiritual goals help us keep our daily focus on an enthusiastic commitment to God and His purposes.

If you have emotional, financial, family, health, academic, or physical goals, now's the time to add spiritual goals to your list. God-given spiritual goals can easily develop as you take time to pray and reflect on His direction for your daily life. If you're unsure of what God has for you, then striking your arrows begins by asking God what He would want you to do.

Spiritual goals are important because they keep you from aimlessly living each day without a spiritual focus. These goals can help you live with purpose and intentionality. They can help clarify the intersection of your passion and skills so you'll readily see how to step into God-given opportunities. In reality, God wants you to continually seek ways to make your mark on those around you, just as Jesus did.

Jesus told us He came to seek and save those who were spiritually lost.[122] He didn't come to "be available" in case anyone decided they'd like to put their faith in God. No, Jesus sought out people. He was on the pursuit, looking for anyone who would willingly follow Him. Likewise, having our eyes open and our ears attentive to the opportunities God presents will help us strike our arrows. In any given moment, you never know what God might do!

A Million Souls

You've probably heard before that one of the keys to accomplishing goals is to keep them in front of you all the time. Studies suggest that those who write down their goals will have the most success at achieving them. In fact, a writer at *Inc.* magazine says that people are 42 percent more likely to achieve their goals if they're written down.[123] That simple act alone gives you a higher likelihood of actually accomplishing your goals.

Writing down your goals means you can visually see them. They're not just saved in some folder on your computer or stored only in your brain. They're out in front of you, and this is important, because our actions are affected by what we see. You're more likely to produce results when you see what you have to do versus just thinking about it. Hence, there's a clear advantage to writing down your goals, including spiritual goals.

This reality became most evident to me on the first day of my sophomore year at Oral Roberts University. My new friend Dominic Russo had arrived as a freshman. We both landed on the fifth floor of Wesley Hall, just a few doors down from each other. Having grown up in ministry homes, we had a similar upbringing, we easily connected, and we quickly became good friends.

Dominic had a heart for people and wanted to make a big impact on the world. Many of the students had a passion to change their worlds, but Dominic was different. He actually had a plan to do it. In fact, it wasn't a theoretical dream for him. He actively put passion into practice all the time.

Everywhere he went, Dominic looked for opportunities for God to use him—a college freshman looking to make his mark in the world. If he was in a restaurant, he made it a point to steer the conversation with servers toward spiritual matters. When hanging out with buddies in the dorm, he looked to find ways to pray with them or encourage them. He had compassion for people, and he wanted to view people the way God sees them.

His life challenged many of the guys on our floor. But that wasn't what left the biggest impression in my mind. His example to others was great, but the future life he planned for himself is what stood out most to me. Dominic had a spiritual goal. He desired to see one million people come to Christ through his efforts for the Lord. Yes, you read that right. One million lives! That's a lot of people—more than the entire population in seventy-six different countries.[124] Yet Dominic wanted to see it happen.

I can still picture this goal typed on a plain piece of white printer paper. Dominic taped it up on the cream cinder block wall in his dorm room. It simply read, in a large font: "1,000,000 souls." It was a goal that had the potential to change history for so many people. Dominic saw it every day, and so did everyone else on the floor. We all knew his spiritual goal, and we were cheering him on.

Since those college days, it's been amazing to see just how God has used Dominic to launch various ministries and initiatives to reach people. By the young age of twenty, Dominic founded Missions.Me and began organizing strategic outreach campaigns in cities across Latin America. In the first fifteen years since its inception, Missions.Me held fifty-nine successful large-scale outreaches in cities across the world.

One particular outreach with an incredible impact was the "1Nation1Day" initiative in Honduras. During a week in late July 2013, that outreach alone reached more than one million Hondurans, and the national newspapers declared, "We Have a New Honduras!"[125] All this happened because Dominic passionately pursued his spiritual goals and took every chance he could to strike his arrows. Having that written goal kept his focus on ways he could make his mark for the kingdom.

You may not have such a lofty goal. What's most important is that you identify your God-given goals and keep them in front of you.

If you haven't yet created spiritual goals, take a moment and ask God to give you clarity on what these could be. God will give you ideas if you ask Him. They might be as simple as calling a friend and inviting them to lunch, or as crazy as reaching one million people. Once a goal has developed, write it down. Keep it before you as you persistently strike your arrows to attain that goal and step into what God has for you.

Initiating New Opportunities

David and Lois Rust owned and operated a chicken farm in southern Indiana. Started by David's family in 1939, Rose Acre

Farms experienced great success in the years that followed. Each year the business continued to expand, so they started acquiring more land and built additional farms throughout the United States.

Rose Acre Farms became an industry leader, and it's still one of America's largest egg producers, with seventeen facilities in eight states.[126] That's quite an operation.

Selling people eggs wasn't their only contribution to society. Starting in 1980, they made a decision to put a Bible verse on their egg cartons as a way to give a message of hope to people.[127] If you've ever purchased a dozen Goldhen eggs from Aldi, then you've likely seen Psalm 118:24 printed inside the carton. This small-town farm, which grew into an egg-producing machine, has shared a Bible verse with millions of people around the world.

God can use a simple verse on an egg carton to encourage the discouraged, give hope to the hopeless, bring healing to one's pain, and produce joy amid sorrow. You never know who might read it at just the right moment, and God will use it to speak to them. What if this company didn't put that verse on there? God certainly could use another means to speak to a person, but why not use an egg company to do so?

Rose Acre Farms took an active approach to spread joy to their customer base by sharing a message from God's Word. You might not have a huge platform, network, or sphere of influence like Rose Acre Farms, but that doesn't excuse you from the necessity to proactively pursue ways to make a difference.

Arrow strikers seek ways to do more for God. They're proactive in their approach. No doubt God wants you to capitalize on opportunities that come to you, but that doesn't mean you must wait for those moments. God always has something special He's wanting to do through you. He wants you to look intently, listen carefully, and leverage opportunities that you discover. Your proactive pursuit of God's daily destiny will equip you to step into all He has for your life.

> *Your proactive pursuit of God's daily destiny will equip you to step into all He has for your life.*

One More

The Bible tells us that God can do "immeasurably more than all we ask or imagine."[128] His infinite power and ability to work in a given situation go way beyond our human comprehension. This means that every time we take one more step into what God has for our lives, God can exponentially multiply it in ways we may never even know.

As my friend Chris Railey once put it, "God can do immeasurably more with your one more."[129] Think about that for a moment. You may not feel like one additional act of kindness, generosity, or encouragement will actually do much, but when we understand that each singular act is immeasurably multiplied, that changes things.

Do you think making a card game would really help people's marriages? Can an eighteen-year-old student truly reach a million people? Would putting a Bible verse inside an egg carton actually encourage someone?

Absolutely!

That's the power of the "one more." One more conversation. One more prayer. One more idea. One more donation. One more act of kindness. One more note of encouragement. One more…

If Israel's King Jehoash had gone a little further, responding more quickly and effectively to the opportunity before him, he would have seen even greater and bigger victories for God's people. What action could you take today to strike your arrows one more time? What's one more thing you can pursue with which God will do immeasurably more?

All it takes is your willingness to seek out one more opportunity. Don't try to do everything. Just try to do something. As nineteenth-century author and historian Edward Everett Hale once said,

> I am only one, but I am one. I cannot do everything,
> but I can do something. And what I can do, I ought
> to do. And what I ought to do, by the grace of God,
> I shall do.[130]

God will help you as you proactively pursue your next opportunity.

CHAPTER 16

GIVE IT "GOD'S ALL"

14:26:04.

That's how many hours it took for the Hoyt men to cross the finish line in the 1989 Hawaii Ironman Triathlon. An amazing feat, it was the first time a father-son duo completed the race in a unique capacity.

The journey began in 1962 when Dick Hoyt's son Rick was born with cerebral palsy. Doctors suggested he would remain in an unresponsive wakefulness state his entire life, but the Hoyts believed they could defy this reality. And they did. Rick learned to communicate using an interactive computer. He graduated from high school and earned a degree from Boston University.

Despite his circumstances, he was a high achiever, following the footsteps of his father. Over the years, the two men would compete together in distance running events. Dick would push Rick in a wheelchair while running anything from a 5K to a marathon. After much success, they decided to start competing in triathlons, where they also experienced incredible accomplishments.

This led them to the 1989 Hawaii Ironman Triathlon, a grueling 2.4-mile swim, 112-mile bike ride, and a 26.2-mile run. *Triathlete* magazine described the Hoyts' astonishing feat:

> After pulling Rick in a raft through 2.4 miles in 1:54:06, they got on the bike. Their bike weighed 76 pounds, Rick weighed in at 125 and Dick was a lean and mean 175. Don't try this at home. Dick was propelling a not-very-aerodynamic 376 pounds through the lava fields in 8:01:30 before pushing Rick to a 4:30:27 marathon to finish in an unfathomable time of 14:26:04.[131]

Yes, they actually completed it. Rick did the entire race with his father, achieving one of the best photo finishes of all time.

We gain a powerful lesson from their inspiring, jaw-dropping physical performances. The only way Rick could achieve such victory was by relying on his father's strength to complete the race. Had it not been for their unique partnership, none of their achievements would be possible. And yet because of the father's physical effort and the son's willingness to participate, these men were victorious. As a result, the Hoyts were inducted into the Triathlon Hall of Fame.[132]

Our human efforts won't achieve much without our heavenly Father's strength. He powers us through to the finish line each and every day. Only through Him can we actually make a difference and see daily victories throughout the opportunities that come our way.

Elisha Versus Jehoash

As you think about the account of Elisha and Jehoash, there's an interesting juxtaposition between the individuals. It gives us a great lesson in perseverance and dependence on God as we strive to give our best for Him.

Jehoash was much younger and healthier than Elisha, but he was weaker in faith and didn't give his best effort. While he could have struck the arrows more times, he didn't. His lackadaisical effort was the result of trying to do it on his own. It was *his* bow and *his* quiver of arrows. Maybe he'd recently been in battle. Maybe his arms were tired. Maybe he was tired. Even though the power of God symbolically was given to the king through the placing of Elisha's hands on his hands, Jehoash did only what *he* could do. And human effort always falls short of God's ability.

Then we have Elisha, who was in his eighties. He was extremely sick and approaching death, yet he still allowed God to use him to the very end—by giving an encouraging word, by imparting the power of God to the king, literally doing all he could for God in those last moments of his life on Earth—ultimately believing that God would give Israel the victory.

In the same way, God wants to grant you the power and ability necessary to accomplish what He has placed in your heart to do. No matter how big or small the opportunities you have throughout any given day, God wants to help you make the biggest difference possible. He has His arms around you, He has given you His power, and He wants to help you.

One of the most encouraging and most often quoted verses in all the Bible is this: "For nothing is impossible with God."[133]

We often think of this verse as it relates to God's awe-inspiring supernatural ability to do whatever we put our minds to. And yet we have to remember that the possibilities are endless with—and *only* with—God. Whatever effort we put forth is nothing unless He is in it.

It's His power at work, not our own strength. Just like Rick, whose father pushed him in race after race, our heavenly Father is the one who empowers us. The Bible tells us that God's power "is at work within us."[134] He'll do immeasurably more than we could ever imagine as He imparts His power to us.

Your Essential Equipment

Among the many challenges during World War II was the need for technological advances. With global supply lines shutting down, the United States military was forced to innovate. They developed specialized boats, vehicles, and aircraft to help them navigate the difficult terrain. They perfected a new synthetic rubber for tanks, aircraft, footwear, clothing, and equipment. And they even developed a new product to protect their ammunition.

Since the weather conditions and humidity varied in the regions where they fought, these conditions greatly affected the military's ammunition cases. Ammunition that was repeatedly exposed to high humidity and moisture would become corroded, and the powder ruined. Preventing this humidity was an essential priority, because they needed to preserve the ammunition as long as possible.

Then Johnson & Johnson's Permacel division invented a new

product that drastically changed the military's efficiency. Taping the cases with a brand-new product nicknamed "duck tape" (a name later evolving into "duct tape") eliminated moisture and ammunition waste. It was a revolutionary advancement at the time. This simple tweak ultimately helped the United States in winning the war.[135]

In the psalms, David says, "Bless the LORD, who is my rock. He gives me strength for war and skill for battle."[136] As we look to rely on God's strength in the spiritual battle, a question we might ask is this: What does it look like to rely on God's strength? The answer lies in the type of equipment we use—the secret weapons God gives to believers to accomplish His purposes.

The apostle Paul gives a vivid illustration of the believers' equipment for God's daily assignments. He called it the "armor of God."[137] This is new equipment given to believers upon salvation, and it increases their capacity to accomplish the mission of God. This armor helps us every day as we dress for the spiritual battle. It's the equipment we need to live out our daily lives with purpose and intentionality. It also helps us stand firm in moments of weakness or opposition.

God has designed "armor" to help us fulfill what He wants us to do. Here's the essential equipment He wants you to wear as you step into what He has for you: committing to truth, living a righteous life, walking in the peace of God, living with faith, and relying on God through prayer and the Word.[138] That's what maximizes your impact and positions you to strike your arrows. That's the life God wants to use.

This equipment is His. These are His weapons. Yet He wants us to have them. He wants us to "take the sword of the Spirit, which is the word of God," and to "pray in the Spirit at all times and on every occasion."[139] In other words, you can win each day as you fight using God's strength, through prayer and dependence on His Word. That's how the battle's won.

When Jesus ascended to heaven, I'm sure guys like Peter wanted to go on a rampage. They could have charged ahead, ready to take on the world. They knew their assignment from God was to carry out what Jesus had begun. But if they did that, it would have been in their own strength and according to their own desires and emotions.

Jesus instead told them to wait for the Holy Spirit to come.[140] They needed to know what dependence on the Holy Spirit looked like after Jesus's departure. They needed to know that this was His strength equipping them to accomplish what He'd designed for them to do. Otherwise, Jesus knew that when difficulties arose, the disciples wouldn't have the vigor on their own to withstand the pressure in the moment.

In the same way, we have power through the Holy Spirit to accomplish what He assigns us to do.[141] Our job is to rely on His power and not our own strength. This takes willingness and discipline, because our human tendency is to rely on ourselves instead.

But when relying on God's strength and power, we still ought to give our best human effort. It doesn't mean our actions are meaningless, nor does it mean we shouldn't work hard. In fact, the example from the apostle Paul tells us quite the opposite. As he labored to reach others and share the gospel, he said, "That's why I work and struggle so hard, depending on Christ's mighty power that works within me."[142]

At the end of the day, remember that this is God's battle, not ours. We're soldiers in His army, following His direction and fulfilling the assignments He places before us. We win the battle by relying on God and giving Him our best each day.

The Multiplied Meal

After the 7.0 magnitude earthquake in Port-Au-Prince, Haiti, on January 12, 2010, people all over the world came together to help provide relief to that country. The news highlighted some of the many things people were doing to make a difference. Movie stars, athletes, doctors, first responders, and average folks all united to help. Everyone's economic status, stage of life, and cultural differences meant nothing in that moment. All that mattered was meeting the needs of the Haitian people.

One news story featured Connor, a nine-year-old arrow striker from Allen, Texas. After seeing an image of a Haitian father holding his deceased baby, Connor wanted to do something. With the help of Connor's mother, he wrote these words on a coffee can wrapped in yellow construction paper: "Please Help Haiti." Connor then asked family and friends for donations, and he went door to door raising funds from neighbors to provide support for the Salvation Army.[143]

Conner seized the opportunity. He did what he could—with the little knowledge, skill, and influence he had at age nine—in order to help people in a unique situation.

This reminds me of another young boy highlighted in the Bible. He, too, made a difference with what little he had to offer. This significant moment in Jesus's ministry displayed a boy's willingness to strike his arrows.

After a full day of speaking to people, healing the sick, and ministering to a huge crowd, it was dinner time. But rather than send everyone home, Jesus wanted to display His marvelous power and build their faith by miraculously feeding everyone, right there.

While the disciples were confused as to how this would work logistically (and financially), Andrew found a young boy who had five barley loaves and two fish.[144] If this growing young boy was anything like my son, you would think he'd want to hoard the food to himself. But that's not what happened.

Instead, we discover this young boy willingly gave his food to Jesus. I can just picture Jesus bending down to the boy's level, taking the food from him, and whispering with a quick wink, "Watch this!" Upon giving thanks to God, Jesus multiplied the food, and everyone ate until they were full. John tells us that when all was said and done, "about five thousand men had eaten from those five loaves, in addition to all the women and children."[145]

> When we give God our efforts, no matter how big or small, He can exponentially multiply our impact and influence.

When we give God our efforts, no matter how big or small, He can exponentially multiply our impact and influence. The key is that we actually have to let God do the work. He'll multiply our acts of kindness, words of encouragement, and daily opportunities into a much greater impact than we could ever achieve on our own.

God doesn't need a big effort to do big things. Instead, He takes the little you have to offer and magnifies it into extraordinary outcomes—if you're simply willing to let Him do His work.

Truthfully, our small efforts won't really have much impact in our own strength. That's why we give our efforts to God each day. We act not on our own accord but on His accord. We use all of *His* power throughout our everyday lives, and He takes those actions and multiplies them as He sees fit.

Since every person's path is different, your job is simply to give God what you can do, and He'll take care of the rest. As we allow Him to hop in the driver's seat, He'll steer the vehicle of our lives where He wants it to go.

Have you found yourself trying too hard to accomplish things on your own?

Always remember: Your human effort will never accomplish what God has intended. Rather, when we give it "God's all," He shows up in unthinkable ways. Just like Rick Hoyt did with his father, may you run the race of life under the direction and power of our heavenly Father. Give what you can to God and watch Him exponentially multiply it in ways you never would have expected.

CHAPTER 17

RUN TO WIN

The book *Unbroken* is a powerful biographical sketch of the incredible life lived by Louis Zamperini, who survived war and torture in World War II. Prior to enlisting in the army, he attended the University of Southern California on a track scholarship. He also competed in the 1936 Olympic Games in Berlin, Germany, where he finished in eighth place in the 5,000-meter race.

Upon joining the military, this strong and talented young man had no idea how life-altering that decision would be.

While on a mission on May 27, 1943, mechanical difficulties caused his bomber to crash in the Pacific Ocean. He miraculously survived the crash and swam to a nearby raft for safety. However, that was just the beginning of a long journey ahead. After floating on the raft for forty-seven days, he and a comrade were eventually captured and tortured by the Japanese for the next two years. He overcame incredible odds and persevered through immense opposition, eventually being freed as the war concluded.

A few years later, Louis committed his life to God at an evangelistic crusade led by Billy Graham. Following his born-again experience, Louis forgave his captors, and the nightmares he had experienced immediately ceased.

Much can be learned from his willingness to forgive the unimaginable, and his life is an inspiration of perseverance and dedication still decades later.[146]

Louis's life is reminiscent of a man in the Old Testament who also overcame a difficult set of circumstances. Although a completely different situation, Jabez was born into a pretty hopeless environment. The Old Testament describes how his birth caused much pain for his mother, so she named him Jabez, which means "distress" or "pain."

In those days, the name of a person defined who they were. Throughout his entire upbringing, he was known as Pain, which is certainly not the best identity a person could desire, as you can imagine. And yet, as Jabez grew up, he didn't allow this to stop him from living a life of purpose.

You see, although Jabez's name described pain and sorrow, he was known as strong and honorable. He prayed that God would bless him and extend his world. He wanted increased territory and influence, and God gave it to him.[147]

In the same way, God has already given you a purpose. He has already defined who you are. You haven't failed too many times. You're not in the wrong career. You're not too young or too old. You're right where God has you for this very moment, and it's time to simply take what you have and give it now to Him.

God wants you to strike your arrows because He has a purpose for you each day. Another day of life means He has more

He wants to do through you. In other words, He's not done with you yet.

No one knows the day or the hour when any of our lives will conclude on Earth. Our job is simply to focus each day on His eternal purposes and look for ways to strike our arrows.

Are you ready to let Him use you in even greater ways?

As was true for Jabez, the blessing is not in how you're labeled. The blessing is a result of your obedience to what God has asked you to do. It's a matter of taking what God has put before you and faithfully giving it your best effort. There's great personal blessing in doing all you can for God.

Your Biography

Someday your life will have a biography. It might not be in written form, but all of us will leave behind a legacy. Wouldn't it be great if the biography of your life could inspire others?

God hopes you'll focus on what matters most to Him, where nothing takes precedence over His desires for your daily life. Your service for God on Earth will inspire others to also

> *Your service for God on Earth will inspire others to also live out their faith.*

live out their faith. In the end, God will abundantly bless you as you seek to obey His leading each day. And the best part is that your life will also be a blessing to others.

In reality, our actions, words, and deeds can powerfully impact others. While no one's perfect, God will honor our faithful attempts to live out our faith with passion and enthusiasm. Your act of kindness just might help someone feel cared for and loved. Your uplifting compliment to someone could give them the confidence they need today. The way you live your life may motivate someone to put their faith in God. You have an opportunity to be a blessing to others, and it starts today.

What can you do today to start moving forward into what God has next for you?

If you've held back from stepping into God-given opportunities, now is the time to get started. The inspirational life is one that strikes arrows whenever possible.

The truth is, you can make a difference. Even if you lack gifts and talents or have little knowledge of the Bible, God still hopes to use your life in ways far greater than you can imagine. It doesn't matter how many times you may have messed up. God still wants to use you in amazing ways.

People may not notice the ways you serve, give, and fulfill God-given opportunities, but God always does, and He's including those things in your biography. He sees every act of kindness, every encouraging word, and every prayer you pray. He knows exactly where you are right now, and He's ready for you to do even more for Him. Your time is short, and much work is yet to be done to advance His purposes in people's lives.

Always remember: It doesn't matter what we bring to the table. As the Bible says, "Commit your actions to the LORD, and your plans will succeed."[148] When we regularly commit our efforts to God, He takes care of the rest. Just like with the boy who brought the five loaves and two fish—it wasn't much, but wow, it had huge success! That's what arrow striking will do. As you take what you have and make the best of it, and fully surrender it to God, He'll make it succeed as He sees fit. And that's all that matters.

In the words of the great American tennis player, Arthur Ashe, "Start where you are. Use what you have. Do what you can."[149] That's the inspirational life of an arrow striker.

Eternal Pine Leaves

First-century athletes went into strict training for a crown made of pine leaves. These were the most coveted honors in the whole Greek world. This was a big deal, just like the shiny gold, silver, or bronze medals are for Olympians today.

The apostle Paul appealed to this understanding of a running competition when he encouraged the Corinthian church in how to live out their faith:

> Don't you realize that in a race everyone runs, but only one person gets the prize? So run to win! All athletes are disciplined in their training. They do it to win a prize that will fade away, but we do it for an eternal prize. So I run with purpose in every step.[150]

Paul acknowledged that the rewards from a physical race don't last forever, unlike the reward we receive based on our spiritual race. That reward is eternal.

Paul had purpose behind what he did. There was a goal—an end result he longed to achieve. He kept his eyes on an eternal reward and his priorities in proper alignment. Paul focused on what mattered most. He saw the finish line in his future, and he knew that what he focused on now would determine how he'd finish in the end.

That's why in his letter to the Philippians, Paul wrote, "I press on toward the goal to win the prize for which God has called me heavenward in Christ Jesus."[151] God wanted Paul to win—and He wants *you* to win.

God desires to know you deeply. Your life matters to Him. He longs for an intimate relationship with you, and He plans to use your life. You've been uniquely gifted by God so that you can play a part in His eternal purposes.

As you run to win, you'll not only experience wonderful blessing now, but you'll also receive a heavenly reward for a life well lived. In the end, you'll be able to echo these words of Paul:

> I have fought the good fight, I have finished the race, I have kept the faith. Now there is in store for me the crown of righteousness, which the Lord, the righteous Judge, will award to me on that day—and not only to me, but also to all who have longed for his appearing.[152]

Rise Up

University of Minnesota's Heather Dorniden had a historic finish in a 2008 Big Ten indoor track event. With just one lap left in the 600-meter final, she fell on the track, shifting her position from first to last place. However, she instantly got up to chase the pack of runners who had built a significant lead over her.

In a wild sequence of events, she caught up and passed her first opponent. Her momentum was building. The fans were cheering. She kept closing the gap between the others in front of her. As she rounded the final curve, she heard the in-house announcer exclaim, "Watch out for Heather Dorniden!"

She thought, *Yeah, watch out! I'm coming!* The adrenaline gave her an incredible surge of energy as she pressed for the finish line. As she waited for the times and names to come up on the video board, she was shocked to discover she'd officially edged out the others, winning the race by four-hundredths of a second.[153]

She later wrote about her stunning victory: "I always tell people this race isn't just about never giving up. It's about discovering what you're capable of when you're given the opportunity to rise above adversity."[154]

Now it's *your* race. This is your moment.

As long as you have breath, there's still time to pick up steam. Even if the race hasn't gone as you thought. Even if you tripped up more than you'd like. Even if you don't think it's worth racing anymore. Even if you haven't seen God work like you hoped.

God is in heaven right now cheering you on. He's saying, "Watch out! Look who's coming! You can do it! Get back up! Finish the race! Go all out! I'm with you! I will help you!"

Now is your time to get in stride and strike your arrows. God has gifted you with talents, abilities, resources, and opportunities. He has something special for you *today*. Just as the prophet Nathan told King David, "Do all that is in your heart, for God is with you."[155]

Heaven's Affirmation

May we always remember that none of us will face eternity before God with a perfect track record. We all have confessions of failure and regret, but our Judge on that day will also be our Savior. Our God's love, mercy, forgiveness, and grace are abundant.

Strike your arrows while you can. Leave a legacy for those who follow you. And as you do, never forget God's tenacious love for you and His promise to supply your every need. May you one day hear His personal affirmation for your lifetime of commitment, sacrifice, and service. In the meantime, may you increasingly sense His love, joy, and peace in your life as you embrace His leading now. Give your all from this day forward, and hold nothing back in your service to God so that when you stand before God in the end, you'll hear, "Well done, my good and faithful servant."[156]

> Give your all from this day forward, and hold nothing back in your service to God.

In life, it's not how you start that matters. It's how you finish. Go all out for God. Passionately pursue Him. Live strong as you fight in the spiritual battle from this point forward. May you run to win.

As Paul concluded in his letter to the Colossians, so I urge you as well: "See to it that you complete the work you have received in the Lord."[157]

You are a God-anointed Arrow Striker. Now is your time. Today is your day. Grab your arrows. Let the striking begin. And whatever you do, don't stop.

CONCLUSION

How did God speak to you as you read this book?

There's no right or wrong answer to that. Everything's on the table. I'd love to hear about any way in which God is motivating you to greater Christian commitment. Send me an email to share what's on your heart. I read and respond to everyone personally, and I'd love to hear from you.

Email: jonathan@jonathanhardy.org

ACKNOWLEDGMENTS

I want to thank my heavenly Father for His unending love, mercy, and grace as I strive to strike my arrows for His glory. This book was birthed in my heart through His leading a long time ago. I'm thankful for His patience with me over the many years it took me to put it all together.

Thank you, Ashley—my amazing wife and best friend. You worked equally as hard to make this book a reality. Your faithful love, constant support, incredible passion, and creative feedback have encouraged me more than you'll probably ever know.

I also want to thank my parents, Dick and Pat Hardy. Much of what has been instilled in this book is a result of your years of investment in my life.

To those who meticulously critiqued, edited, and proofed this book: Danielle, Justin, Ryan, Shelly, Thomas, Tim, Todd, and Tom. Your input significantly improved the content of this book. Thank you!

Finally, a special thanks goes to all those who have encouraged me throughout the writing process. Your enthusiasm for this book is contagious!

NOTES

1. 2 Kings 13:7
2. 2 Kings 13:15-17
3. 2 Kings 13:18-20
4. Ephesians 6:11-12
5. John Lindell, *Soul Set Free: Why Grace Is More Liberating Than You Believe* (Lake Mary, Florida: Charisma House, 2019), 79.
6. Colossians 4:17
7. 1 Peter 5:8
8. "Human Genome Project FAQ," on the website of the National Human Genome Research Institute, at this link: https://www.genome.gov/human-genome-project/Completion-FAQ.
9. Ephesians 2:10, NLT
10. These gifts include those listed in Romans 12:6-8 and 1 Corinthians 12:7-10.
11. Exodus 31:3-5, ESV
12. As quoted by Angela Ruth in "Thomas Edison—Don't Miss an Opportunity," *DUE* website, at: https://due.com/blog/thomas-edison-dont-miss-an-opportunity.
13. Mark Batterson, *Primal: A Quest for the Lost Soul of Christianity* (Colorado Springs: Multnomah, 2010), 45-46.
14. "Top Ten Best Selling Books of All Time," on the Rankings website, at this link: https://www.rankings.com/books-sales-worldwide.
15. "Box Office History for Peter Jackson's Lord of the Rings Movies," on *The Numbers* website at this link: https://www.the-numbers.com/movies/franchise/Peter-Jacksons-Lord-of-the-Rings#tab=summary.
16. Matthew Miller, Dorothy Pomerantz, Lacey Rose, Lauren Streib, and Marie Thibault, "Dead Celebs," on the *Forbes* website at this link: https://archive.vn/20120731182631/http://www.forbes.com/2009/10/27/top-earning-dead-celebrities-list-dead-celebs-09-entertainment_land.html.
17. Justin Taylor, "85 Years Ago Today: J. R. R. Tolkien Convinces C. S. Lewis That Christ Is the True Myth," September 20, 2016, on Taylor's blog at this link: https://www.thegospelcoalition.org/blogs/evangelical-history/85-years-ago-today-j-r-r-tolkien-convinces-c-s-lewis-that-christ-is-the-true-myth.
18. John 1:41
19. Matthew 16:18
20. "History of Amazon" on the *Wikipedia* website, at this link: https://en.wikipedia.org/wiki/History_of_Amazon.

21. "Big Tech Continues Its Surge Ahead of the Rest of the Economy," *New York Times* online, October 29, 2020, at this link: https://www.nytimes.com/2020/10/29/tech-nology/apple-alphabet-facebook-amazon-google-earnings.html.
22. 2 Kings 13:25
23. Matthew 10:8
24. Mark 12:41
25. Mark 12:42
26. Mark 12:43-44
27. Ephesians 2:8-9
28. Romans 10:9, NLT
29. James 2:26
30. Colossians 3:17
31. James 4:14, NLT
32. Colossians 4:5
33. Isaiah 55:8-9
34. "Mordecai Ham" on the *Wikipedia* website, at this link: https://en.wikipedia.org/wiki/Mordecai_Ham.
35. John 9:4
36. Romans 13:11-12, The Message
37. Deuteronomy 6:5
38. Ephesians 6:19-20
39. Joshua 1:9
40. Philippians 1:28
41. Joshua 1:5
42. "Labor Force Characteristics—Hours of Work" item, "Labor Force Statistics from the Current Population Survey," U.S. Bureau of Labor Statistics online, at this link: https://www.bls.gov/cps/lfcharacteristics.htm#hours.
43. "Economic News Release—Table 4. Families with own children: Employment status of parents by age of youngest child and family type, 2019-2020 annual averages," U.S. Bureau of Labor Statistics online, at this link: https://www.bls.gov/news.release/famee.t04.htm.
44. Gretchen Livingston, "About One-Third of U.S. Children Are Living with an Unmarried Parent," on the Pew Research Center website, at this link: https://www.pewresearch.org/fact-tank/2018/04/27/about-one-third-of-u-s-children-are-living-with-an-unmarried-parent.
45. Luke 2:49
46. John 6:38
47. Luke 8:43-47
48. Mark 2:1-12; Luke 5:17-26
49. John 21:25, NLT
50. Mark 10:49
51. Galatians 6:10
52. https://www.worldometers.info/coronavirus/coronavirus-death-toll
53. Psalm 90:12, NLT
54. Mark 2:27, NLT
55. https://www.soulshepherding.org/pastors-under-stress

56. Ephesians 4:12, NLT
57. Matthew 17:20
58. J. D. Greear, *Stop Asking Jesus into Your Heart: How to Know for Sure You Are Saved* (Nashville: B&H Books, 2013), 63-64.
59. Luke 17:5
60. Proverbs 27:17
61. An example of this can be found in Psalm 34.
62. Aaron Berry, "What Does Jesus Mean by 'Faith as Small as a Mustard Seed'?" on the *Crosswalk* website, at this link: https://www.crosswalk.com/faith/bible-study/what-does-jesus-mean-by-faith-as-small-as-a-mustard-seed.html.
63. "Kurt Warner," *Britannica* online, at this link: https://www.britannica.com/biography/Kurt-Warner.
64. https://www.krqe.com/sports/the-big-game/after-super-bowl-success-kurt-warner-builds-his-legacy-off-the-football-field
65. 1 Samuel 17:36
66. 1 Samuel 17:34-37
67. 1 Peter 3:15
68. https://lullabyofhope.org
69. "Vancouver's Bannister and Landy Statue and the Miracle Mile," on the *BC Write* website, November 21, 2019, at this link: https://bcwrite.com/2019/11/01/vancouvers-bannister-and-landy-statue-and-the-miracle-mile. An archived film of the TV coverage recorded the full race is at this link: https://www.youtube.com/watch?v=Z-0VMZqOcDM4.
70. Romans 12:6, NLT
71. "Some Interesting Self Esteem Statistics and Facts You Might Not Be Aware Of," on the *Self-Esteem-School* website, at this link: https://www.self-esteem-school.com/self-esteem-statistics.html.
72. 2 Corinthians 5:17, ESV
73. Romans 8:14-16
74. Romans 8:17
75. Romans 12:2, NLT
76. Ephesians 4:12, NLT
77. 1 Corinthians 12:18, NLT
78. 1 Corinthians 12:22, NLT
79. 1 Peter 1:13, NLT
80. Matthew 26:36-46; Mark 14:32-42; Luke 22:40-46
81. Proverbs 13:20, ESV
82. Proverbs 15:22
83. Luke 17:33
84. Matthew 16:24; Mark 8:34; Luke 9:23
85. Philippians 2:3-4
86. Andrew Murray, *Absolute Surrender: The Blessedness of Forsaking All and Following Christ* (New Kensington, Pennsylvania: Whitaker House, 1981; originally published 1895), 26.
87. 1 Corinthians 10:24

88. Jenny Santi, "The Secret to Happiness Is Helping Others," *Time* magazine online, at this link: https://time.com/collection/guide-to-happiness/4070299/secret-to-happiness.

89. Philippians 2:5-8

90. Oswald Chambers, "Gracious Uncertainty," *My Utmost for His Highest* online, at this link: https://utmost.org/gracious-uncertainty.

91. "Eye of the Tiger" on the *Wikipedia* website, at this link: https://en.wikipedia.org/wiki/Eye_of_the_Tiger.

92. 1 Corinthians 9:26-27

93. 2 Corinthians 4:17-18

94. Philippians 3:13-14

95. Hebrews 12:1

96. Matthew 6:33, NLT

97. Philippians 4:19

98. Romans 8:1

99. 2 Corinthians 3:17

100. Galatians 5:7

101. Luke 5:16

102. Luke 6:12

103. Mark 6:45-46

104. Mark 3:14

105. Acts 4:13, NLT

106. Proverbs 29:18, The Message

107. Galatians 5:25, NLT

108. https://datacommons.org/ranking/LifeExpectancy_Person/Country/northamerica?h=country%2FUSA

109. https://www.statista.com/statistics/274513/life-expectancy-in-north-america

110. Leigh Campbell, "We've Broken Down Your Entire Life into Years Spent Doing Tasks," *HuffPost* online, October 19, 2017, at this link: https://www.huffingtonpost.com.au/2017/10/18/weve-broken-down-your-entire-life-into-years-spent-doing-tasks_a_23248153.

111. John 15:1-2

112. Andrew Murray, *Absolute Surrender*, 8.

113. "Steve Prefontaine" on the *Wikipedia* website, at this link: https://en.wikipedia.org/wiki/Steve_Prefontaine.

114. "Steve Prefontaine Quotes," *Successories* online, at this link: https://www.successories.com/iquote/author/12774/steve-prefontaine-quotes/1.

115. "Top-20 Richest NBA Players of All Time," *SportyTell* online, at this link: https://sportytell.com/nba/richest-nba-players.

116. Philippians 2:7

117. Acts 20:24, NLT

118. Philippians 4:8, NLT

119. Colossians 3:2, NLT

120. Romans 12:2

121. https://becausemarriagematters.com/connectioncards

122. Luke 19:10

NOTES

123. Peter Economy, "This Is the Way You Need to Write Down Your Goals for Faster Success," *Inc.* online, at this link: https://www.inc.com/peter-economy/this-is-way-you-need-to-write-down-your-goals-for-faster-success.html.
124. https://www.worldometers.info/world-population/population-by-country
125. "The Story of 1Nation1Day" and "Honduras," video clips, *Missions.Me* online, at this link: https://missions.me/1nation1day.
126. https://www.goodegg.com/about-us/company-history
127. https://www.aldireviewer.com/goldhen-eggs
128. Ephesians 3:20
129. Chris Railey, sermon on Ephesians 3:20 at Summit Park Church in Lee's Summit, Missouri, October 25, 2020.
130. https://www.goodreads.com/quotes/472462-i-am-only-one-but-i-am-one-i-cannot
131. Bob Babbitt, "From 5K to Ironman, Team Hoyt's Unbreakable Bond," *Triathlete* online, March 18, 2021, at this link: https://www.triathlete.com/culture/people/recalled-from-5k-to-ironman-team-hoyt-is-unstoppable. Originally published in the November/December 2013 issue of *Inside Triathlon* magazine.
132. Garry Brown, "As Team Hoyt, Father and Son Inducted into Triathlon Hall of Fame," *MassLive* online, February 23, 2020, at this link: https://www.masslive.com/sports/2020/02/as-team-hoyt-father-and-son-inducted-into-triathlon-hall-of-fame.html.
133. Luke 1:37
134. Ephesians 3:20
135. "Innovating for Victory," on the website for the National WWII Museum in New Orleans, at this link: https://www.nationalww2museum.org/war/articles/innovating-victory.
136. Psalm 144:1, NLT
137. Ephesians 6:11
138. Ephesians 6:14-18
139. Ephesians 6:17-18, NLT
140. Acts 1:4
141. Acts 1:8
142. Colossians 1:29, NLT
143. Kim Nguyen, "Allen Boy Raises Funds for Earthquake Victims," *Allen American* (Allen, Texas) website, January 20, 2010, at this link: https://starlocalmedia.com/allenamerican/news/allen-boy-raises-funds-for-earthquake-victims/article_af12538e-c84b-5704-b2da-cc8966ed64db.html.
144. John 6:9
145. Matthew 14:21, NLT
146. "Louis Zamperini" on the *Wikipedia* website, at this link: https://en.wikipedia.org/wiki/Louis_Zamperini.
147. 1 Chronicles 4:10
148. Proverbs 16:3, NLT
149. Arthur Ashe, as quoted in the *Self Journal*, 2015-2016, page 89.
150. 1 Corinthians 9:24-26, NLT
151. Philippians 3:14
152. 2 Timothy 4:7-8

153. "Heather Dorniden Wins the Race," YouTube video clip at this link: https://www.youtube.com/watch?v=g9rUUz8cMDM.
154. Brent Yarina, "A Race to Remember: 'I Had No Idea I Fell Like That' in Inspirational 2008 Run," Big Ten Network website, June 3, 2015, at this link: https://btn.com/2015/06/03/a-race-to-remember-i-had-no-idea-i-fell-like-that-in-inspirational-2008-run.
155. 1 Chronicles 17:2, ESV
156. Matthew 25:21,23, NLT
157. Colossians 4:17

ABOUT THE AUTHOR

Jonathan Hardy is the co-founder of Leaders.Church, the online streaming service to help pastors master their ministry and leadership skills. He is also the co-founder of Church University, the online education platform for pastors and ministry leaders.

Over the past 15 years, Jonathan and his wife, Ashley, served on the pastoral staff of James River Church in Springfield, Missouri and Summit Park Church in Lee's Summit, Missouri. They have a passion to help the local church reach their community so more people can experience all God has for them. Jonathan and Ashley have three children: Emery, Axel, and Fia.

www.jonathanhardy.org

twitter.com/JonathanLHardy

facebook.com/JonathanLHardy

instagram.com/JonathanLHardy

DOWNLOAD THE AUDIOBOOK FREE!

As a special thanks for buying my book, I want to give you the Audiobook version entirely free.

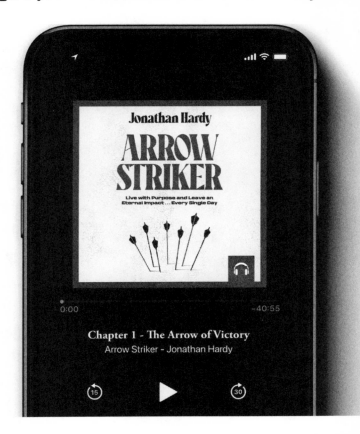

DOWNLOAD HERE:

www.arrowstriker.com/audio
or scan the QR code.

ALSO AVAILABLE

ARROW STRIKER
Video Bible Study

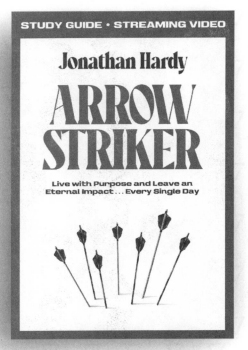

Engage with Jonathan Hardy's *Arrow Striker* in a small group setting as you discover together how to live with purpose and leave an eternal impact . . . every single day!

This study guide includes:

- Individual access to streaming video sessions
- A guide for leading small group discussion
- Study guide for deeper reflection between sessions

To learn more, go to: www.arrowstriker.com/videos

SCAN ME

THERE'S MORE FOR YOU.

Check out these other ways to stay engaged with *ARROW STRIKER* and JONATHAN HARDY:

SPEAKING ENGAGEMENTS

Invite Jonathan to speak at your church or event!

Learn More at:
www.jonathanhardy.org

OTHER WAYS TO CONNECT

www.arrowstriker.com
Twitter: @JonathanLHardy
Instagram: @JonathanLHardy
Facebook: @JonathanLHardy

Leaders.Church

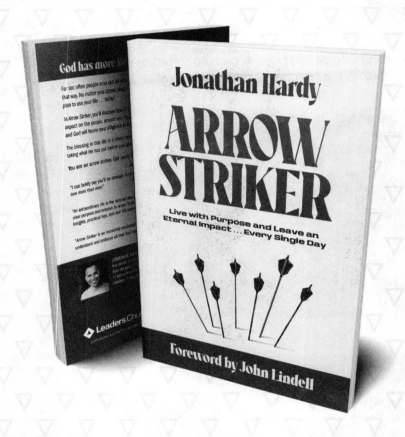